Serving the Marginalized through Design Education

Design education and practice are inherently social from process to implementation. This book explores the transformation in design education, as educators prepare their students to address complex social design problems for all people in society.

This seven-chapter volume provides the reader with a range of viewpoints on the role of design education in shaping the world. The book begins with the overarching potential of design to address the needs of an increasingly complex society and the importance of worldview that underpins education methodology. Each chapter addresses a context that varies by discipline – architecture, graphic, packaging and interior design – and location – Nigeria, Canada, Lebanon, UK and USA. The authors pull back the curtain on their educational methods and provide the reader with a candid view of their teaching outcomes. The needs of the marginalized – victims of Asian hate, students with dyslexia, tomato farmers and even design students themselves – are brought into focus here. These specific places and peoples provide a design context that can be translated to other situations in design education and practice.

Design educators and practitioners of many design disciplines will benefit from the philosophical discussions and the practical education examples offered here. This volume can contribute to transforming design education that will one day transform design practice to place a greater emphasis on the needs of the forgotten in society.

Steven B. Webber was a design practitioner for over 10 years prior to teaching interior design at Florida State University where he has been an educator for 12 years. His areas of teaching span the curriculum, including first year undergraduate students in the introductory course, junior-level undergraduate students in construction documentation and construction technologies and the senior-level undergraduate and graduate-level design studio capstone courses. Research areas include design pedagogy, emotional intelligence, empathy and systemizing. In 2023–2025 Steve will serve in executive leadership roles (president-elect, president and past-president) of the Interior Design Educators Council.

Routledge Focus on Design Pedagogy
Series Editor: Graham Cairns

The Routledge Focus on Design Pedagogy series provides the reader with the latest scholarship for instructors who educate designers. The series publishes research from across the globe and covers areas as diverse as beginning design and foundational design, architecture, product design, interior design, fashion design, landscape architecture, urban design, and architectural conservation and historic preservation. By making these studies available to the worldwide academic community, the series aims to promote quality design education.

Progressive Studio Pedagogy
Examples from Architecture and Allied Design Fields
Edited by Charlie Smith

Emerging Practices in Architectural Pedagogy
Accommodating an Uncertain Future
Edited by Laura Sanderson and Sally Stone

Teaching Architecture(s) in the Post-Covid Era
The New Age of Digital Design
Edited by Sadiyah Geyer

Cultural Awareness in Teaching Art and Design
Edited by Kirsty Macari

Serving the Marginalized through Design Education
Edited by Steven B. Webber

For more information about this series, please visit: https://www.routledge.com/architecture/series/RFDP

Serving the Marginalized through Design Education

Edited by Steven B. Webber

Routledge
Taylor & Francis Group

LONDON AND NEW YORK

First published 2025
by Routledge
4 Park Square, Milton Park, Abingdon, Oxon OX14 4RN

and by Routledge
605 Third Avenue, New York, NY 10158

Routledge is an imprint of the Taylor & Francis Group, an informa business

British Library Cataloguing-in-Publication Data
A catalogue record for this book is available from the British Library

ISBN: 978-1-032-70244-5 (hbk)
ISBN: 978-1-032-70590-3 (pbk)
ISBN: 978-1-032-70592-7 (ebk)

DOI: 10.4324/9781032705927

Typeset in Times New Roman
by Apex CoVantage, LLC

The editor and authors thank Graham Cairns of Architecture, Media, Politics, and Society for his tireless efforts to elevate the role and importance of design education to positively transform our future. May the efforts of AMPS continue to unite the global design education community and bear fruit for all peoples for generations to come.

Thank you to Caroline Church and Meghna Rodborne of Taylor and Francis for advocating in favour of this work and for ushering us through the writing, revision, and production process.

Contents

Figures

Contributors

Beth Sennett has worked in education for over 22 years as a primary teacher, educational developer, education lecturer and neurodiversity specialist. She is passionate about inclusive and transformative pedagogies, evolving from her experiences as a neurodivergent individual. Her research explores the work of educationalist Paulo Freire to support dyslexic students in higher education. Beth also learns from critical educators Bell Hooks and Beverly Tatum, along with the amazing students she works with daily. When not working, Beth loves to bake cakes. She lives with her husband and a cat called Korg.

June He is Assistant Professor of Product Design at Drexel University. She is a multifaceted designer and artist. Her passion and work focus on aging and relevant design innovation, participatory design methods, and a collaborative, cross-cultural design process with diverse participants. She uses empathic modeling and participatory design to help increase mobility for students with disabilities and explores the design opportunity at the intersection of gender, immigrant and cultural identity. June is currently leading Aging + Design courses and research projects at Drexel University.

Siobhan Barry is Senior Lecturer at Manchester School of Architecture, a joint school between Manchester University and Manchester Metropolitan University. She is an internationally respected academic and researcher in the fields of bioclimatic architecture, aviation and exhibition design. She has worked regularly with the National Trust in designing pavilion exhibitions for public interaction and engagement across a number of historic sites. Siobhan presents internationally and has consulted on sustainable development strategies for both architectural practice and government.

Aziza Cyamani is Assistant Professor of Product Design in the Department of Interior Design at the University of Nebraska-Lincoln. She is a multidisciplinary designer with experience in product development, visual communication and sustainable systems. Her interests center upon the integration of crosscutting topics in product design education, particularly focusing on sustainability, object meaning in diverse cultures and social impacts of artifacts.

Charles Nwaizu joined the Department of Food Science and Technology as Assistant Professor of Practice in Summer 2020. He is strongly concerned about subjects on rethinking teaching and learning process that is centrally pinned on empathy – a student-focused pedagogical approach to the learning process.

Andrea Sosa Fontaine is Assistant Professor of Interior Design at Kent State University. She has practiced interior design in both Canada and the US, where she designed schools, community centers, workplaces and healthcare facilities. She understands that the root of good design is through community engagement. Andrea teaches her students diverse and non-linear methods of design to foster the tailoring of design practices to unique community needs. Her research has focused on modifications to the practices of design to foster equity and respect for future memory in the built environment.

Tina Patel is Assistant Professor to the Interior Design Program at Kent State University. Her work examines the intersection of people, processes and the built environment. She has presented at conferences and published her research on learning environments for neurodiversity and underrepresented groups, impact of evolving workplaces on behavior and design pedagogy. Tina has established partnerships with community leaders, non-profits and design practices dedicated to empowering communities to expand on teaching methodologies centered on community engagement. Her pedagogy aims to sharpen students' understanding of others with different realities by utilizing ongoing social and economic issues affecting our communities.

Inge Roecker is the founder of AIR studio whose work is focused on multiunit housing, sustainable practices and architecture's relationship to social and cultural issues, such as aging populations and inclusive design. Inge is Associate Professor of Architecture at the University of British Columbia, where she specializes in studios focused on community partnerships and housing. She is the co-founder of the interdisciplinary research collective, Design for Inclusion, which explores resilience in urban communities through architectural inquiry.

Introduction

Steven B. Webber

Design for Humanity

Design impacts all areas of life and improves the lives of human beings that engage with the designed object, place or experience.[1] Design is both functional and beautiful with a specific context, culture and people that it is intended to serve. Design and the process that creates the design is an indispensable service to humanity as the design professional prioritizes "meeting the needs of the present without compromising the ability of future generations to meet their own needs".[2] Expressed another way,

> Designers approach the solution from the vantage point of the end-user, seeking to optimise for the specific needs and capabilities of that individual or group. Designers strive to "do more with less," they maximise economy (of materials, of investment, of energy, etc.) through creativity and ingenuity; this idea is central to design.

Design impacts humanity in a variety of ways requiring depth of expertise resulting in discipline specialties. These specialties include the built environment design (landscape, architecture, interiors), objects and product design (industrial, furniture, fashion, textiles) and experiential design (graphics, web, print and events). Each of these disciplines overlap in the multidisciplinary design world we inhabit. For example, furniture is often designed as individual or coordinated objects, and draperies are designed as textiles while they both fit into the design of building interiors, and graphic design or branding is incorporated into packaging, product and landscape design to name a few examples. Coupled with our increasingly complex world, design disciplines have become more specialized over time.

Design disciplines have been pursuing human- or user-centered design since the 1960s. Human-centered design finds its conceptual roots in the work of John E. Arnold,[3] professor of engineering and business administration at Stanford University 1957–63, John Kling is credited with first using the term user-centered design in 1977,[4] and Donald Norman brought the concept into

DOI: 10.4324/9781032705927-1

the mainstream with *The Psychology of Everyday Things*[5] published in 1988 and later renamed *The Design of Everyday Things*. The International Organization for Standardization defines human-centered design this way,[6]

> Human-centred design is an approach to interactive systems development that aims to make systems usable and useful by focusing on the users, their needs and requirements, and by applying human factors/ergonomics, and *usability* knowledge and techniques. This approach enhances effectiveness and efficiency, improves human well-being, user satisfaction, *accessibility* and sustainability; and counteracts possible adverse effects of use on human health, safety and *performance*.

The power to do good on behalf of the end-user is in the hands of the designer. The 2017 World Design Summit in Montreal was an international gathering of diverse design disciplines that advocated for the critical role of design and the influence of designers. The representatives in attendance committed to many resolutions regarding the importance of design, including

> To inspire designers – too long the servants of producers – to better serve humanity as the ambassadors of the end-users: the citizens of the world.
> All people deserve to live in a well-designed world.[7]

To achieve this resolution, design disciplines must embrace a model of authentic, meaningful and sustainable human-centered design education practices that meet the needs of all, including the underserved.

Worldview in Pedagogy

In the spirit of collaboration, the six chapters in this work present techniques and outcomes geared towards design education transformation. The goal is to better serve all of humanity, including the forgotten, marginalized, and those separated by geography, life stage, culture, ability, and economy. As design education experiences a transformation, design practice could follow, leading to improved quality of life for a growing number of people.

This issue begins with the importance of worldview, the power of theory setting the stage for education and practice. Paulo Freire's theories of education discussed in Chapter One is the context for this discussion. Paulo Freire is a well-recognized education philosopher whose ideas provide much of the foundation for current-day critical pedagogy theory. Critical pedagogy finds close allies with critical race theory and other critical social theories that have been growing in popularity within academic circles for several decades and have recently risen to prominence in public circles of cultural and political discourse. Freire authored *Pedagogy of the Oppressed*,[8] a highly influential book that posits much of the traditional educational models that have been in use for over a century are founded upon the power of the oppressor or instructor over the oppressed, students. As posited by the oppressor-oppressed educational worldview, injustice is perpetuated, even multiplied, and learning is less effective for the disadvantaged under the traditional educational models that identify the educator as the "depositor" of knowledge into students' minds.

As Freire's theories have become more accepted in education and have been put into practice over the last several decades, the theory, writings and results have been critiqued by many. For a compilation of some of these criticisms, look to the work of John Ohliger,[9] where he outlines the views of many scholars. The topics of criticism include

- The overly complex writing style often veils the meaning from the audience, including the oppressed.[10]
- The notion of "conscientization" or "consciousness raising" accentuates the class divide between the elite and oppressed by elevating the elite further as the holders of liberation.[11]
- The ambiguous use of religious symbolism is missing a clear and practical exhortation.[12]
- The presentation of the evils of the oppressor-oppressed relationship is devoid of an improved replacement or utopian vision.[13]
- The advocacy of increased literacy as a means of liberation of the oppressed is frequently paired with political ideology which invites skepticism on the intent of expanded literacy – is it actually an attempt to indoctrinate the vulnerable?[14]
- Freire's apparent preference for theory over practical application of his philosophies contributes to a sense of contradiction within his writings and interviews.[15]
- The teacher-student relationship is viewed as a pseudo-non-hierarchical endeavor that could too easily result in political and social indoctrination.[16]
- Freire's language is often male-centric, and his descriptions of liberation and manhood are often intrinsically linked, resulting in the alienation of women from his philosophy.[17]
- The divide between Freire's theory and practical action steps dilutes the transferability between people groups separated by geography, culture and time.[18]

Over the decades, some passionate supporters of Freire's work have tempered their views as Freire's theories have evolved and have been put into practice. One example is Blanca Facundo, author of the monograph *Freire-inspired programs in the United States and Puerto Rico: a critical evaluation.*[19] The work describes Paulo Freire as a human being, the cultural context of Brazil in his early life during which his work was conceived, the perception of Freire and his work in the USA, the advocates and executors of Freire's philosophies in the USA and Puerto Rico and the results of their work. The breadth of the writing provides additional context and a balanced view of the practical outcomes of Freire's theories. Jeff Zacharakis-Jutz, reviewer of Facundo's work states, "If students in adult education are required to read *Pedagogy of the Oppressed*, then they should also read this monograph".[20]

This complementary view of Freire's work is offered here because all teaching methodology is founded upon a worldview which shapes culture and history for the next generation. Educators should carefully consider the impact upon students of the pedagogical/andragogical worldview behind their methods. Awareness of negative outcomes and contrarian opinions can help avoid repeating past mistakes. Great educators often seek to hone their craft of teaching by considering counterpoint arguments followed by a critical self-evaluation of their practices. Blanca Facundo states it this way,

> If we find that we are or were unclear about the meaning and objectives of the theory upon which our educational activities were or are being based, and have accepted it as inherently relevant to our work, what kind of clarity can we have when evaluating the process and outcomes of our programs? Particularly when we are supposed to be acting and critically reflecting upon our actions![21]

The intent here is not to add further criticism to Freire's work, but to raise awareness that multiple viewpoints exist on this topic, and others like it, and to call the reader to develop their own well-informed opinion on the worldviews that form the foundation of many current pedagogical and andragogical methods.

Overview of Book Chapter Contents

Chapter One

Beth Sennett offers observations of learning transformations through the educational lens of oppression by Paulo Freire in Chapter One. Paulo Freire offers a transformational view of pedagogical practice by bringing awareness to the power differential between the oppressor and oppressed in the traditional classroom. Building upon this awareness, Freire calls for a transformed educational system that is made in collaboration with the oppressed such that the result redistributes the power equally between teacher and student. Problem posing rather than depositing knowledge into students' minds (the banking system of education described by Freire) offers students and teachers the opportunity to discuss and analyze ideas prior to dictating solutions. The process of critical thinking and challenging assumptions is embedded in this process which can lead to previously unseen solutions and an educational environment that liberates the oppressed.

Sennett offers three examples of applying Freire's theories where educators can work to create a learning environment that helps students become agents of positive change in their world. First, Dyslexics Untie provided a way for university students with dyslexia to communicate in a workshop setting with one another and others their experiences in school and society. The methodology behind the workshop is explained and student outcomes through their testimonials are examined. Second, MEG, Morph Education Group, was created in collaboration with a neurodivergent student with the purpose of developing a more inclusive education praxis. Outcomes are examined in context with the scale of the effort with an eye towards future development. Lastly, Breaking Through, a program at a UK university that unpacks students' encounters with racism on their campus and in classes is discussed and analyzed. Observations of the process and outcomes include the impact of the unique remote learning process during the pandemic, and students' interactions with one another and the instructor team. While this chapter does not directly address a deign education context, it offers methods of engaging students as stakeholders in their education that educators from all design disciplines could benefit from.

Chapter Two

Juanjuan (June) He offers an insider's look at the Aging & Design course at Drexel University in Philadelphia, USA, in the post-pandemic world. The experiential design course engaged graphic design students and locals in an interactive learning environment that sought to address real-life design problems of aging Asian people. Experiential design is user-centered graphic design that seeks to create or enhance positive experiences for those who engage with the graphic design, product, or built environment. The chapter provides discussion on the pedagogical theories underpinning the course, the three unique roles of the design educator, and the learning and design outcomes of the course.

The author discusses the learning theories that provide structural support for the course approach and context, including Vygotsky's social constructivism theory and transformative learning theory. The notions of empathic design, equity-centered design and experiential learning led the author to engage in a community-based participatory design project in the Aging & Design course at Drexel. These theories and design processes possess common characteristics that provide an interlocking web to support the pedagogical approach in the course.

The author provides a personal reflection upon her roles and experiences through the lens of a tripartite persona of the educator: design facilitator, design acupuncturist, and design therapist. The design facilitator brings the design students into contact with real-life users with complex and tangible design problems who can benefit from the design solutions proposed by the students. The design acupuncturist is responsible to focus on the physical processes of the course, such as course structure, schedule and location of meetings, while dismantling barriers whenever possible so the participants can focus on the design process. The design therapist complements the acupuncturist by addressing the emotional qualities of the course, such as student and stakeholder fulfillment, collaboration and communication. Each of these roles must work in concert for any design course, and the importance and complexity of the instructor excelling in each of these areas increases when projects extend beyond the hypothetical to include actual clients, or users, in the design process alongside students.

In the context of the supporting theories and instructor roles, the course structure, methods and design outcomes provide the reader with approaches to replicate and areas to build upon. Examples of student work and student reflections provide engaging color for this innovative course. To conclude, the author provides a transparent view of areas for improvement for future coursework that could contribute to instructional guidelines for other educators or contexts.

Chapter Three

Siobhan Barry, of Manchester School of Architecture, describes the importance and growth of student resilience in architectural education in context with a live project of pavilions for the Winter Garden at Dunham Massey, a UK National Trust house in Cheshire, England. A live project is an academic design project that includes some combination of real clients, users, place and can also involve some manner of construction or making, and in this context all of these characteristics were present. Resiliency has always been an important part of students transforming into practicing design professionals, but the COVID-19 pandemic and accompanying social isolation has emphasized the needs of young people to develop resiliency in a meaningful and inclusive way. The biosocial education model and Engeström's activity theory provide context for the evaluation of student resiliency in the context of this student learning experience.

The author provides a detailed account of the course structure and outcomes. Starting with an overview of the course pace and project brief and progressing through the construction process, the reader will be able to see the complex strategy and tactics used to complete a live project of this magnitude. The discussion on design and construction outcomes alongside student growth outcomes are supported through photographs and resilience analysis using two methods: systemic resilience by design and systemic resilience by intervention. Building upon lessons learned from pandemic teaching and learning, it is clear that resiliency should not simply be a by-product of design education, but something that is intentionally taught and celebrated.

Chapter Four

Aziza Cyamani, Charles Chioma Nwaizu and Noor Al Maamari of University of Nebraska in the USA, advocate for practice-based learning methods to improve student learning outcomes. They make the case that the market demands higher transdisciplinary experience and soft skills in collaboration, communication, and critical thinking. The authors tackled student learning needs while simultaneously addressing the complex real-life problem of food insecurity, specifically postharvest loss of tomatoes in Nigeria, through a product packaging design course. Design for sustainability and design at the base of the pyramid provide the conceptual basis for the design problem. The closely related pedagogical hot topics of project-based learning, problem-based learning, and practice-based learning are each addressed in turn as they provide the theoretical framework supporting the course methodology.

The course planning project programming are described to set the context of the project outcomes and data analysis. The student work outcomes discussion includes design images and reflection upon the viability of the proposals alongside improvements for future pedagogical application. The pilot study that accompanied the course results in a preliminary data analysis at the current stage of development that can be used to develop a framework for future research to evaluate the effectiveness of this practice-based learning approach. The study was able to identify valuable traits to develop in students – a systems thinking mindset, problem-solving skills and contextual/cultural sensitivity.

Chapter Five

Andrea Sosa Fontaine and Tina Patel call design educators to embrace the complexities of cross-border student collaboration while tackling complex design problems geared towards meeting the needs of marginalized populations. The authors recount the triumphs and struggles of *After Care*, an elective interior design studio course where students from Kent State University (Ohio, USA) and Lebanese American University (Beirut, Lebanon) collaborated on design project with one another. The chapter begins with an analysis of interior design curricula and an analysis of learners and educators through the lenses of localism vs. globalism, multiculturalism, role of empathy in design and self-reflection at the educator, student and curricula structure levels. The notion of aftercare in this context is defined as first recognizing the long-term impact of life events on people, space and communities followed by an empathetic design response.

Based upon the foundation laid in the first portion of the chapter, the authors move forward to explain and analyze the course and its outcomes, recognizing that certain circumstances (such as a global pandemic) exerted influence upon the curriculum. The course began with bringing KSU and

LAU students together virtually followed by the students sending one another digital care packages. This experience allowed the students to build empathy for one another that would serve as the foundation for their working relationships. The reflection exercise that followed allowed the students to become producers rather than simply consumers of knowledge. The second portion of the course utilized a design charrette to create an encounter between the interior design students and a complex design problem where empathy would be required to meet the needs of a marginalized group of people. In this case, the user group was focused on Asian Americans in Chinatown New York City who had been targets of xenophobia during the COVID-19 pandemic. Again, student reflections were integrated into the course and provided students the opportunity to create knowledge rather than simply receive knowledge. The authors close the chapter reflecting upon the course successes and areas for improvement, followed by a charge to all design educators to weave empathy into their design curricula.

Chapter Six

Authors Inge Roecker and Andrea Hoff of the University of British Columbia identify the misalignment, or *mismatch*, between design education and practice versus priorities of inclusion. Architectural education is identified as an exclusive rather than inclusive system which perpetuates the same notions of exclusivity in practice even to the point of housing designs following similar exclusive ideals. The growing movement of empathy building among students and educators and practitioners and those who use their designs offers a remedy to the lack of inclusivity. The COVID-19 pandemic and the immediate shift to online learning emphasized the divide within architectural education. The focus becomes realignment of priorities in architecture education and practice towards a care-centered model – students in education and spatial users in practice (i.e., the marginalized in institutional housing) – that relies upon building empathy to be successful.

The course analyzed in this chapter prioritized creating innovative housing solutions for the marginalized using innovative design processes in the studio which relied upon innovative pedagogical approaches. In other words, the same old architectural education approach would result in the same flawed housing design outcomes, and the authors committed to make every possible effort for their students create new housing models. The studio course was structured in three phases: Research (storytelling and case study analysis), Innovation (Innovation Mapping), and Prototype (Designing & Prototyping). Within each phase guest lectures by experts outside of architecture were utilized to engage with students to further their understanding on a particular relevant topic. The chapter provides an informative view of three student projects: a tofu factory with multigenerational housing, an adaptable senior living environment and a community-centered grocery store. The authors close with a call for architecture educators to transform the world of design by unlocking their students' desires to create for the betterment of all humanity.

Conclusion

In summary, this book advocates for the authority and responsibility of design educators to transform their pedagogical approach to prepare the next genera- tion of designers to positively transform their future world. This future could be founded on empathy for one's fellow human being where design outcomes provide a better life for those who inhabit spaces, use products and engage in life-changing design experiences. The designer of the future will be called to address problems of complexity we cannot yet imagine, but a worldview founded on empathy will guide them through those challenges.

Notes

1 "What Is Design?" International Council of Design, n.d., https://www. theicod.org/en/professional-design/what-is-design/what-is-design.
2 United Nations Brundtland Commission, "Report of the World Commission on Environment and Development: Our Common Future," 1987, accessed January 30, 2024, http://www.un-documents.net/our-common-future.pdf.
3 John E. Arnold and William J. Clancey, "Creative Engineering Promoting Innovation by Thinking Differently," 2016, https://stacks.stanford.edu/file/ druid:jb100vs5745/Creative%20Engineering%20-%20John%20E.%20 Arnold.pdf.
4 Rob Kling, "The Organizational Context of User-Centered Software Designs," *Management Information Systems Quarterly* 1, no. 4 (December 1, 1977): 41, https://doi.org/10.2307/249021.
5 Donald A. Norman, *The Psychology of Everyday Things* (New York: Basic Books, 1988).
6 International Organization for Standardization, "ISO 9241–210:2019(En) Ergonomics of Human-system Interaction – Part 210: Human-centred Design for Interactive Systems," 2019, accessed February 18, 2024, https://www.iso.org/obp/ui/#iso:std:iso:9241:-210:ed-2:v1:en.
7 Montreal World Design Summit, "Montreal Design Declaration," 2017, https://www.theicod.org/storage/app/media/01_The%20Council/06_ Montreal%20Design%20Declaration/Montreal_Design_Declaration_ 2017_WEB.pdf.
8 Paulo Freiré, *Pedagogy of the Oppressed* (New York: Continuum, 1970).
9 John Ohliger, "Critical Views of Paulo Freire's Work," 1995, accessed February 18, 2024, https://www.bmartin.cc/dissent/documents/Facundo/ Ohliger1.html#I.
10 William Ayers, "Review of a Pedagogy for Liberation," *Teachers College Record* 89, no. 1 (1987): 162–63.
11 John L. Elias and Sharan B. Merriam, *Philosophical Foundations of Adult Education*, 1980, http://ci.nii.ac.jp/ncid/BA25901733.

12 Harold Beder, "Review of Conscientization and Deschooling by John L. Elias," *Adult Education* 27, no. 4 (1976).
13 William S. Griffith, *Paulo Freire*, ed. Stanley Grabowski (Syracuse: Syracuse University Publications in Continuing Education, 1972).
14 Sandra Stotsky, "On Literacy Anthologies and Adult Education: A Critical Perspective," *College English* (December 1990): 916–23.
15 David Nasaw, "Reconsidering Freire," *Liberation*, September 1974.
16 John L. Elias, *Paulo Freire* (Malabar: Krieger Publishing, 1994).
17 bell hooks, Speaking About Paulo Freire in *Paulo Freire*, eds. Peter McLaren and Peter Leonard (Oxfordshire: Routledge, 1993).
18 R. Oliveira, D. Dominice, and P. Dominice, *The Pedagogy of the Oppressed: The Oppression of Pedagogy* (Institute of Cultural Action, 1974).
19 Blanca Facundo, "Freire-inspired Programs in the United States and Puerto Rico: A Critical Evaluation," 1984, accessed February 19, 2024, https://www.bmartin.cc/dissent/documents/Facundo/Facundo.html.
20 Jeff Zacharakis-Jutz, "Review of Issues for an Evaluation of Freire-Inspired Programs in the United States and Puerto Rico," *Adult Literacy and Basic Education* 10, no. 3 (1986).
21 Facundo, "Freire-inspired Programs in the United States and Puerto Rico."

Bibliography

Arnold, John E., and William J. Clancey. "Creative Engineering Promoting Innovation by Thinking Differently." 2016. http://purl.stanford.edu/jb100vs5745
Ayers, William. "Review of a Pedagogy for Liberation." *Teachers College Record* 89, no. 1 (1987): 162–63.
Beder, Harold. "Review of Conscientization and Deschooling by John L. Elias." *Adult Education* 27, no. 4 (1976).
Elias, John L. *Paulo Freire*. Malabar: Krieger Publishing, 1994.
Elias, John L., and Sharan B. Merriam. *Philosophical Foundations of Adult Education*. 1980. http://ci.nii.ac.jp/ncid/BA25901733.
Facundo, Blanca. "Freire-inspired Programs in the United States and Puerto Rico: A Critical Evaluation." 1984. Accessed February 19, 2024. https://www.bmartin.cc/dissent/documents/Facundo/Facundo.html.
Freire, Paulo. *Pedagogy of the Oppressed*. New York: Continuum, 1970.
Griffith, William S. *Paulo Freire*. Edited by Stanley Grabowski. Syracuse: Syracuse University Publications in Continuing Education, 1972.
hooks, bell. Speaking about Paulo Freire in *Paulo Freire*. Edited by Peter McLaren and Peter Leonard. Oxfordshire: Routledge, 1993.
International Council of Design. "What Is Design?" n.d. https://www.theicod.org/en/professional-design/what-is-design/what-is-design.
International Organization for Standardization. "ISO 9241–210:2019(En) Ergonomics of Human-system Interaction – Part 210: Human-centred Design for Interactive Systems." 2019. Accessed February 18, 2024. https://www.iso.org/obp/ui/#iso:std:iso:9241:-210:ed-2:v1:en.
Kling, Rob. "The Organizational Context of User-centered Software Designs." *MIS Quarterly* (1977): 41–52.

Montreal World Design Summit. "Montreal Design Declaration." 2017. https://www.theicod.org/storage/app/media/01_The%20Council/06_Montreal%20Design%20Declaration/Montreal_Design_Declaration_2017_WEB.pdf.

Nasaw, David. "Reconsidering Freire." *Liberation*, September/October 1974.

Norman, Donald A. *The Psychology of Everyday Things*. New York: Basic Books, 1988.

Ohliger, John. "Critical Views of Paulo Freire's Work." 1995. Accessed February 18, 2024. https://www.bmartin.cc/dissent/documents/Facundo/Ohliger1.html#I.

Oliveira, R., D. Dominice, and P. Dominice. *The Pedagogy of the Oppressed: The Oppression of Pedagogy*. Institute of Cultural Action, 1974.

Stotsky, Sandra. "On Literacy Anthologies and Adult Education: A Critical Perspective." *College English* (December 1990): 916–23.

United Nations Brundtland Commission. "Report of the World Commission on Environment and Development: Our Common Future." 1987. Accessed January 30, 2024. http://www.un-documents.net/our-common-future.pdf.

Zacharakis-Jutz, Jeff. "Review of Issues for an Evaluation of Freire-Inspired Programs in the United States and Puerto Rico." *Adult Literacy and Basic Education* 10, no. 3 (1986).

1   Learning Through Freire

Applying Transformative Pedagogy to Transform All Learners

Beth Sennett

Introduction

a [person] who transforms the world is transformed.[1]

Brazilian educationalist Paulo Freire sought to understand the performative nature of education. He recognized how education, as a practice, can never be neutral; it always functions as either a means to bring about conformity or freedom.[2] As Giroux discusses, for Freire, pedagogy was not a method but a "political and moral practice".[3] Therefore, educators are presented with a choice: to choose to assimilate students into the world as it is or to help them to become active subjects engaged in constructing the future.[4] Through exploring Freire's work and its application to a series of case studies, this chapter will illustrate how Freire's pedagogy can support the latter.

The chapter begins by exploring how power works through the education system. This power can be wielded by the elite to maintain systems of oppression, or it can be harnessed by critical educators and students to transform and liberate. Freire's transformative pedagogy will then be outlined by introducing the philosophies that underpin his work while exploring how these ideas are essential in enabling design educators to nurture a critical, socially engaged mindset with their students. The chapter will conclude by providing three practical examples of how Freire's transformative pedagogy can be applied to different educational contexts. The structure of this chapter reflects Freire's insistence that educators must find a "marriage between theory and methods, but theory always precedes methods".[5]

Higher Education

The history of higher education is grounded in the idea of education as a public good, enriching society by developing intellectual thinking, engaging in research to solve societal problems and providing necessary professional

DOI: 10.4324/9781032705927-2

knowledge and skills.[6] However, as Giroux[7] states, higher education has now been reduced to a "private good" with institutions focusing on maximizing productivity, employability and student (often referred to as customer) satisfaction.[8] Measures of accountability, such as the Teaching Excellence Framework (TEF) in the UK, serve to enforce this approach.[9] While some argue that the TEF gives students a means to make an informed judgment when selecting their university,[10] the TEF's focus on retention, progression to postgraduate study and employability[11] shifts higher education further towards a neoliberal ideology. At the same time, managers (who may have no formal pedagogical background or experience) can reduce education to a process of techniques at the loss of critical pedagogy.[12] Education is then reduced to training, inculcating students for the workplace while ensuring performative measures are reached. Within this climate the practicalities of "what works", are given precedence.[13]

This adulation of marketization then enables the elite to justify the authoritarian education required to maintain their position of dominance. Those in power can define what knowledge, subjects and vocations are valued and which are not. Control over the ontological and epistemological construction of society enables the elite to preserve their position of power.[14] As Freire and Macedo illuminate "To be intellectual one must do exactly what those with the power to define intellectualism do".[15] This tactic can be observed in the UK government's dissolution of the arts and subjects they deem "low value for money",[16] cumulating with the introduction of their term "rip-off university degrees".[17] Discrediting degrees which have creativity and criticality at their core, arguably makes it easier for the elite to ensure education focuses on "the standardization of content, and the transfer of a well-behaved knowledge of results".[18] Education in this form serves to subjugate the masses and maintain the authority of the oppressors as inequalities are reproduced through the education system.[19] Freire warns that this authoritarian approach to education can easily become normalized, blinkering teachers from the reality of oppression and maintaining the illusion of autonomy.[20] He cautions that the invisibility of this approach adds to the difficulty of changing the authoritarian system, as teachers can often "confuse freedom with the maintenance of the status quo".[21]

Oppression

For Freire, the reproduction of inequality through education is part of a much larger system which creates and maintains oppression.[22] He discusses how oppression is produced through the interchange between the superstructure (formed by our history, culture and traditions) and the infrastructure (formed, and reinforced, through policies, systems and procedures). As those in power dictate the creation of policies (which inform practice), Freire argues this enables the elite to maintain oppression through manipulation of the infrastructure

Figure 1.1 The superstructure/infrastructure interaction

(Figure 1.1). Over time, the infrastructure reinforces the superstructure, as ideas and practices become normalized and hence are perceived as a cultural norm. In turn, the rationale and justification for policy creation is reinforced through the elite's control and domination of both politics and the mass media, allowing them to manipulate discourses, giving the elite "the power to define, profile and describe the world".[23]

The power of the infrastructure/superstructure interaction, placates those within it, camouflaging and normalizing oppression.[24] This phenomenon then works to pacify those who are oppressed into believing their situation must be the result of their own perceived inadequacies or a consequence of a pre-determined system that cannot be changed.[25] This process creates a fatalism that Freire refers to as the "culture of silence", where the oppressed accept their situation simply as "the way things are". As Freire says, "their perception of themselves as oppressed is impaired by their submersion in the reality of oppression".[26]

With the infrastructure being both informed by and informing the super-structure, a perpetual cycle is created. Within this process all actions are informed by the oppressive system, while simultaneously also serving to reinforce it. As Freire explains, each time we act (e.g., interact with others, create objects or ideas, etc.) our actions in the world create our culture.[27]

These actions are informed by our prior knowledge, experience and view of the world, so consequently, they create a mirror of what was there before. Therefore, our culture risks becoming domesticating, "a product that is simultaneously capable of conditioning its creator".[28] If human beings continue this process of creating the world uncritically, then oppressive systems will be perpetuated.

The direct role that designers take in creating new products and technologies necessitates their ethical responsibility to transgress these systems of oppression. As Freire suggests, we are not just passive beings; we are active subjects involved in a process of making and re-making this world, a process Freire describes as "humanities ontological vocation".[29] As Freire illuminates "by 'making' we are creating and recreating reality".[30] Consequently, the responsibility of design educators to develop a critical pedagogy that will enable design students to recognize, illuminate, examine and ultimately transgress these oppressive systems, is paramount.

Hope

Freire's tireless dialogical theorizing provides hope, revealing how educators and students can work to facilitate these transformations. Reflecting on how his understanding of higher education has changed over the years, Freire discusses how he once believed social power was solely *reproduced* through the education system, benefiting the elite by maintaining the status quo.[31] Whereas, he later recognized that education and society form a dialectical relationship; therefore, it is precisely *because* power is reproduced through education that critical educators and students are in a unique position to disrupt and redirect that power, enabling it to not just work *on* people to oppress but also *through* them to liberate.[32] The fundamental vocation of designers, to make and recreate the world, makes it especially vital for design educators to engage in a type of critical pedagogy that will enable design students to use that power to unveil and transgress oppression. As Freire reminds us, we are "conditioned but not determined".[33]

However, Freire cautions that, "humanistic education is a utopian project of the dominated and oppressed".[34] Therefore, this transformative action should only be conducted by educators who are willing to transgress the power within their own classrooms, developing an approach with those who are oppressed as active subjects and not "unfortunates".[35] This often requires subverting the established systems of an organization, as to expect institutions themselves, or those who benefit from the status quo, to engage in this work would "be equivalent to asking the dominating class if it is planning a type of education that would rebel against its domination".[36] Therefore, critical educators need to ensure that any approach they take is developed with those who are oppressed by the system, and not those who benefit from the current status quo.

Freire's Pedagogy

For this co-creation to be genuine, Freire consistently reinforces the necessity of creating a pedagogy that is designed *with* the oppressed, situated within their cultural context and developed through an understanding of their lived experience.[37] Therefore, every application of his pedagogy will (and must) be unique. It is for this reason that Freire frequently resisted calls to create a technical guide, believing that this would lead to a mechanistic approach that would only serve to reinforce oppression.[38] Instead, Freire grounded his pedagogical approach around a set of philosophical principles and not a set of instructions, stating, "What I do provide, while avoiding universalizing oppression, is the possibility for the educator to use my discussions and theorizing about oppression and apply them to a specific context".[39]

Co-Creation

The idea of students co-creating curricula has been a prominent idea in higher education in recent years;[40] however, this philosophy formed the foundation of Freire's pedagogy. Freire believes that transformation cannot occur through authoritarian teaching.[41] To develop a subjective and objective reading of the world and expanded worldview, all involved must be equal partners in this process of knowledge creation.[42] No one person can dominate, and no one's voice is invalid. As Freire illuminates "If I am interested in knowing the people's ways of thinking and levels of perception, then the people have to think about their thinking and not be only the objects of my thinking".[43]

This approach is especially important when teachers are working with design students from marginalized groups who have historically been excluded from the process of production.[44] The placatory nature of the culture of silence,[45] combined with exclusion from spaces of knowledge production and the design process,[46] results in many marginalized students lacking faith in their own voice or developing ideas that are perceived by others as radical, when compared to the prevailing dominant system. Only through developing an approach to education that directly and authentically challenges the hegemony of the classroom, can we embrace the diverse experiences required to truly transform the world.

Dialogue

Another key principle of Freire's pedagogy is the necessity to engage students in critical dialogue. Through the exchange, construction and re-construction of ideas, students question and debate reality until a deeper understanding of the world is developed. This process illuminates the construction of oppressive structures, while also revealing opportunities for re-construction. Freire describes how, "all who are involved help each other mutually, growing together in the common effort to understand the reality which they seek to transform".[47]

The opportunity to engage in critical dialogue is especially important for those who have historically been oppressed, to mitigate the effects of the culture of silence. Freire discusses how the oppressed often view the world from a purely objective or purely subjective position, giving them an incomplete view of their situation. For those who only see the world objectively, their conscious awareness of the world is purely an objective copy of how they personally experience it.[48] If they experience oppression, then the world is oppressive, with no possibility for change. Equally, a purely subjective reading of the world risks perceiving a fantasy, built on the myths nurtured by the oppressors.[49] In this state, the oppressed can understand their oppression as resulting from some supernatural force or an act of fate. Both readings of the world lead to fatalism, as there is no possibility for change. However, through engaging in critical dialogue, the oppressed are exposed to realities and perceptions beyond their personal experiences, enabling them to dissect, question and ultimately uncover the structures that maintain oppression. The more someone engages with reality, the more they understand it so that "knowing it better, he or she can transform it".[50] Therefore, impeding dialogue is a tool of the oppressor; engaging in authentic collective dialogue is a tool for transformation.[51]

Problem Posing

To ensure that this dialogue is authentic, ideas must be presented as problems for discussion, rather than facts to be consumed. This problem posing approach acts in opposition to "banking education", where ideas are deposited into students' heads.[52] Students who passively accept these deposits are praised for their academic prowess, while neoliberal performative systems reward teachers who are skilled depositors.[53] Therefore, to truly engage in authentic problem posing dialogue, both students and teachers must work to question their perceived roles along with their ontological and epistemological understanding of the world.[54] Teachers must acknowledge that what they know is just one possible view, and if that viewpoint remains static, then they risk reinforcing authoritarian education. Similarly, students need to recognize that their experience, knowledge and view of the world is equally as valid as that of their teacher's. Freire is often keen to point out that this approach does not deny the existence of the expert but instead recognizes that knowledge can never be static; it is only developed in the dialectic through continued inquiry with the world and with others.[55] Therefore, the ability for teachers to be students and students to be teachers is paramount to Freire's pedagogy. Without this mutual sharing of knowledge, the dialectic is not formed; no new knowledge is created, and transformation cannot occur.

For design students, this problem posing approach is especially important if oppressive structures are to be transformed. With the superstructure/infrastructure interaction normalizing oppressive systems, policies and structures, new designs can often unwittingly build upon and reinforce these systems.

Without engaging in critical conversations which present reality, not as an objective fact but a problem to be investigated, questioned and transformed, design students risk reinforcing existing systems of oppression.

It is important to recognize that these conversations can often be challenging, as they can "unsettle the logic" of the system.[56] However, work by movements such as the Design Justice Network & Tech Won't Build It, are working to unveil the oppression which can often be built into designs when designers fail to critically question reality.[57] For example, designers such as Costanza-Chock and Noble have illuminated the connection between design and power. Constanza-Cook illustrates the example of how the design of millimeter wave scanners (body scanners used in airport security) assume a normative body shape and will flag anybody that differs from this, as a security threat.[58] Therefore, individuals who have a gender identity which differs from the sex they were assigned at birth, anyone who wears a head wrap, such as Muslim women or Sikh men, Black women who may wear their hair high, people who have a different number of limbs or a differently shaped body will frequently be stopped and searched as a result of these machines. Similarly, Noble discusses "algorithmic oppression", highlighting how the algorithms created by Google software engineers for their search engines, reinforce racist and misogynist stereotypes of Black women.[59] She illustrates how in 2011, searches for "Black girls" resulted in pornographic and sexualized images, and how in 2015, Google's algorithm for tagging photos attached the word "apes" and "animals" to images of Black people. These examples illustrate the need for design students to engage in a process of problematizing reality to recognize and mitigate oppressive structures and ensure their work is transformative.

Critical Thinking with Action

Engaging in critical dialogue while problematizing reality, begins a process of critical awakening where students begin to perceive the possibility that reality can be transformed. Critically engaging with the world, makes reality itself "the object of knowledge"[60] as students begin to reveal the social, political and historical context in which situations of oppression exist.[61] Students begin to recognize how reality is constructed, limiting the power of the myths that maintain oppression and revealing the part they can play in actively reconstructing the world. They view reality "not as a closed world from which there is no exit, but as a limiting situation which they can transform".[62] This realization invariably leads to action as students recognize their agency as active subjects in the world. Here begins a cycle of critical reflection with the world and action to transform it. Neither can work in isolation as reflection without action results in nothing more than an "armchair revolution", whereas action without critical reflection runs the risk of perpetuating oppression and replacing one oppressive system with another.[63]

Freire theorizes that engaging in this praxis (the cycle of critical reflection upon the world with action to transform it) leads to a critical awakening, a state of becoming that Freire refers to as conscientização.[64] Once students are engaged in the ongoing process of conscientização, they have the awareness to continue to question the myths of oppression. Critical reflection then becomes a direct threat to neoliberal ideology.[65] As hooks illuminates, when educators are prepared to push the boundaries of education and engage in this cycle, education becomes "the practice of freedom".[66]

Putting Freire into Action

> Those who put my experience into practice must strive to recreate and also rethink my thinking. In so doing, they should bear in mind that no educational practice takes place in a vacuum, only in a real context – historical, economic, political, and not necessarily identical to any other context.[67]

Freire's belief that knowledge should be developed dialectically through questioning, conversation and critical thinking was embodied in his own practice. Throughout his life, he continued to critique his own ideas through dialogue with others.[68] He believed that reading itself should be an act of dialogue between the reader and the author and so advocated that readers of his work should not passively absorb his ideas.[69] Therefore, he consistently encouraged others to "re-think [his] thinking".[70] As previously discussed, Freire believed that this process was vital if educators were to apply his work authentically to their own context and avoid falling into the trap of inadvertently creating an authoritarian form of education, where pedagogy is viewed as a series of instructions that the teacher applies.

This section outlines three occasions where Freire's pedagogy has been adapted to suit the context and the lived experience of the students. Each case study demonstrates the impact of Freire's transformative pedagogy.

Dyslexics Untie

The aim of the Dyslexics Untie group (a name chosen by the students as a dyslexic spelling of Dyslexics Unite) was to provide a space where dyslexic university students could share and discuss their experiences. Freire's pedagogical approach was adapted to create a methodology that had the potential to be transformative.

Students were invited to a preliminary workshop where they collaboratively identified key themes of "being dyslexic". This ensured the starting point for the project was the students' own experiences. This approach to collectively creating themes was important for this cohort of students as those who are neurodivergent often experience a dual stigma which isolates them from both the neurotypical and disabled communities. Slorach explains how the challenges created for neurodivergent people by a system designed for neurotypicals are often unrecognized. This then results in neurodivergent people being blamed when they fail to thrive within these disabling systems.[71] Additionally, within the dis-abled community neurodivergence can often be viewed as not being disabling enough. This dual stigma, combined with the individualized nature of one-to-one support favored by most UK universities, has resulted in many students with dyslexia being isolated from their peers.[72] This isolation then serves to maintain the culture of silence as it prevents the dialogue needed to reveal a shared experience and a new way of perceiving dyslexia.[73]

Therefore, given the impact of the culture of silence on this group, an adapted nominal group technique was employed to provide a safe, non-judgmental and scaffolded approach to collaboratively reveal the themes of "being dyslexic" at a UK university.[74] Students were first invited to complete the phrase "Dyslexia is . . ." by writing their responses on a sticky note. These responses were then grouped by the students, and a theme was attached to each group of words. Once the generative themes were collectively identified, they were then coded as either an image, quote or video and represented back to the students in subsequent sessions, to encourage dialogue. For example, the students identified the theme "difficulty with literacy". Therefore, a series of newspaper headlines were introduced which touted the "disgust" at poor literacy in schools[75] and how this "Cannot Be Tolerated Or Excused".[76] The headlines evoked a discussion of society's perception of those for whom literacy acquisition does not come easily. This led to a historical exploration of literacy (led by two student members who majored in history), to uncover the roots of this perception.

The discussion explored the social dichotomy created in 17th century Britain, where books were read aloud in coffee shops for others to listen to.[77] Consequently, the written word and those who could read, were seen to represent modernity and truth, whereas those who listened were considered uneducated. Verbal knowledge exchange was viewed to be based on superstition and untruths. This discourse then became a mechanism for the elite to justify the exclusion of the "uneducated" or illiterate from political power, maintaining the elite's authority over the masses.[78] With the advent of the industrial revolution, it became necessary for the masses to acquire a basic level of reading, allowing them to follow the written instructions required for them to be effective workers.[79] Critical educators, such as Freire and Meek, argue that this resulted in the teaching of reading becoming a mechanical process which values and rewards accurate decoding, over student's critical engagement with the text (something that could challenge the elite's control over public discourse).[80] Performative measures of accountability, simultaneously label those who do not master this mechanical approach to reading as a failure.[81]

Through critically reflecting on the historical threads informing the newspaper headlines, students were able to uncover how historical and cultural discourses had informed our modern perception of literacy and society's mistrust of those who disrupt the social conventions of reading and writing. Critical engagement with the work of Collinson, whose concept of "lexism" illuminates how a cultural reliance on text-based medium creates dyslexia, enabled students to further disrupt the elite's construction of literacy norms.[82] As Fetterley observes "Literacy is political".[83]

After engaging in these discussions, the group planned what action they wanted to take to disrupt this discourse around literacy, reflecting Freire's assertion that critical reflection must be followed by action.[84] The students chose to hold an event to raise awareness of these issues. The Dyslexics Untie event involved student presentations, information stalls and discussions with attendees. Afterwards, the group reflected on the event's impact and decided to engage in further action. This additional reflection/action cycle resulted in the students liaising with the university library to improve the space for dyslexic learners, along with presenting to educational professionals at a national conference.

Transformation

The transformative impact of the group is evident in both the actions they took (and continue to take) on their objective reality but also in the transformation of their consciousness about the world. This is exemplified through quotes taken from interviews conducted with the students both prior to the project and afterwards. The interviews were analyzed with the students.

In the first interview, before the discussion groups, Kami described the challenge of getting support for her dyslexia at school.

Kami: I remember . . . . it was just "you're not concentrating", "but I'm trying to, believe me, I am". . . . I remember even approaching my year head, and she was like "yeah, well, maybe in college they can test you". . . and even at college they didn't. I approached them. I went straight there like the first couple of days and I said I think I'm dyslexic, can I get a test? And they're "Oh, well, you don't, you don't do an A-Level so there's no point. You don't have an exam".[85]

In this narrative, Kami consistently represents herself as powerless. She looks to her teachers for help yet is consistently given false hope that things will change or told she is the problem as she is "not concentrating". She experiences what Freire refers to as the culture of silence where the oppressed are consistently silenced until they accept their situation as "the way things are" or the result of a deficit in themselves.[86]

When asked in the final interview, after the discussion groups and action, how she would respond to these teachers today, she replies:

Kami: You grow up idolizing these teachers who are teaching you, so you expect them to be like ten out of ten and know everything and it's just like . . . they don't know everything and it's like, well, in that case, they need to educate themselves more.[87]

Her response suggests the erosion of the perceived power of her teachers as she recognizes their fallibility. This shift demonstrates that Kami is developing conscientização; she is starting to recognize social contradictions and question reality.[88]

Jean provides another example of a participant developing a broader understanding of the world. In the first interview, she described multiple perceived deficits within herself which she attributed as the cause of her educational difficulties. Even after her diagnosis of dyslexia, she continued to blame herself, "I guess it was kind of reassuring . . . It was like, there was actually something, in my brain". However, in the final interview, Jean shows a more critical understanding of education when she evokes ideas proposed by Illich,[89] providing a possible solution:

Jean: . . . obviously the school system was built for the majority . . . But if they're [dyslexic students] not made to think like the classroom is the only place that they can learn . . . the school almost acts as a supplement to the ed . . . or like an enabler of education . . . Like there's other ways to educate and the school is just one of them.[90]

This statement shows how Jean is recognizing her ability to transform reality. This continues when she links the inequality she experienced with capitalism.

Jean: I think it's like a feature of a capitalistic culture . . . I think the issue is how fast paced society is . . . So, I think that's maybe why the money is focused on things that go the fastest and in current society that usually correlates with who is neurotypical . . .[91]

The students' desire to transform their objective reality is further exemplified in these quotes from the final interviews, where students discuss changes they have observed or would like to happen.

Debbie: . . . having like a box in the library of colored overlays,. . . which all students could benefit from . . . Like, it's little things . . .[92]

| Jean: | . . .'cause doing the Dyslexics Untie, the meetings before that and meeting new people increases my knowledge of dyslexia, my knowledge of how it is responded to by other people, which then in turn, would impact how I would see it in another person.[93] |
| Andy: | I'd like to think this is a stepping-stone, a laying the foundation brick for something else, to push on forward.[94] |

The students' drive for change continued after the project. Several students stayed in touch and explained how they had developed initiatives in their workplace, which raised awareness of dyslexia and also mental health (a passion of one of the students).

Morph Education Group (MEG)

Morph Education Group (MEG) was co-developed following a request by a student to engage in broader conversations around education that would reflect their experience as a neurodivergent student studying at a UK university. Therefore, MEG was established with the aim of enriching students' understanding of education's function in society and impact on the wider world. As hooks explains, "To educate for freedom, then, we have to challenge and change the way everyone thinks about pedagogical process. This is especially true to students".[95]

As MEG had been requested by a student, it was less formal and had fewer members than the Dyslexic's Untie group. The generative themes for discussion were identified through an initial conversation, where students shared their experiences of education. From this discussion, the students identified themes they wished to explore further in future sessions. Themes included "What is the purpose of education?" and "Why do universities teach through lectures?" Many of the group's members were studying education courses. Consequently, the theories and ideas used to question dominant discourses were introduced by the students during discussions, rather than being used by the facilitator as starting points for dialogue (as happened in the Dyslexic's Untie group). Later sessions were planned and facilitated by students, including discussions on inclusive education.

Transformation

The transformative impact of this group was arguably smaller than the Dyslexics Untie group. This was partly due to the impact of the pandemic which transitioned the group online and diminished the opportunity for students to engage in the action part of the reflection/action cycle. However, the students' enthusiasm to develop and lead their own discussions demonstrates the agency that was developing within the group. Students began to recognize their agency as creators of knowledge and not simply passive receptacles. The group's drive to share their objective experiences while learning from the experiences of others, enabled them to question the perceived wisdom of the established education system and begin to consider an alternative approach. In addition, two members of the group went on to train as teachers and consequently continued their critical engagement with pedagogy outside of the university.

Breaking Through

I developed the Breaking Through group with my colleague, Nicki Northern, as a response to students sharing their experiences of racism at university. The university was situated within a prosperous area of the UK with a predominantly white (94%) population. Only 10% of students identified as being from the Global Majority and only 8% of staff. We recognized that students who reported racism felt that their experiences were often trivialized or dismissed. This perpetuated the culture of silence and exemplified a common tactic of the oppressor, to submerge the developing consciousness of the oppressed.[96] Therefore, we wanted to create a space where students would be heard, where they could engage in authentic conversation around race and interrogate the structures that normalize racism.

The group drew upon Freire's pedagogy while also being influenced by the anti-racist work of bell hooks and Beverly Tatum. Therefore, critical dialogue worked to build community, challenge racist culture and expose how universities reproduce "privileged knowledge and values".[97] The development of Freire's concept of conscientização became a pivotal focus for the group. As Ngugi wa Thiong'o states, domination of a person's "mental universe", controlling how they see themselves and their place in the world, is a vital tool for domination.[98]

In this instance, the generative themes for discussion were discovered dialectically, revealing themselves as the students shared and discussed their stories. The sharing of stories was an important step for this group as stories form a vital part of enabling students of color to affirm their own identity and act as a counternarrative to the stories of the oppressor.[99]

Topics of conversation included performative allyship, decolonizing and cultural appropriation. Facilitation of the conversations required a considered approach. It was important to enable the students time to pause, think and process the experiences others chose to share. This meant being comfortable with the silence often required for this process. Consideration was then given to the themes raised by the speaker so that further questions could be asked to enable the group to uncover the culturally embedded racism that made this reality.

An interesting aspect of Breaking Through was that, like MEG, the discussion moved online during the pandemic. However, this proved beneficial to the group. It was evident during the development of Breaking Through that many students of color felt mistrust in the authenticity of the project. Equally, many white students expressed how they felt they had no right to speak on matters of race. However, when the group moved online, we observed many new members initially joining the group with their video cameras turned off. This allowed students a degree of anonymity until they established they would be affirmed. It was pleasing to note that students would then turn their camera on in subsequent sessions.

Transformation

The transformative impact of the group was evident through ongoing feedback. Students suggested that the greatest strength of the group was (what one student termed) the "non-judgmental, free flowing" aspect. By openly acknowledging the discomfort often felt by both students of color and white students when discussing race, the group was able to engage in brave conversations.[100] This approach enhanced the breadth of critical engagement.[101] In addition, many students spoke of how valuable the group was. One student discussed how they had considered leaving the university before discovering the group. They mentioned that they had been drawn to the university by marketing promotions which alluded to a diverse campus. However, when they arrived, the lack of diversity resulted in an alienating experience. Other students requested a Breaking Through group for alumni as they were keen to continue to engage after completing their course.

Transformation is also evident in the students' impact on their objective reality. Three members of the group became active participants of influential working groups, developed as part of the university's decolonizing strategy to illuminate colonial knowledge and practices embedded in curricula, policy and practice. The students' engagement with conscientização meant that they were able to recognize and expose elements of tokenism or performative allyship within these groups, enhancing the anti-racist work throughout the university. Another member presented at a conference and told their story of starting university and experiencing a very different campus to the image of diversity portrayed on university marketing material. In addition, members of Breaking Through have joined anti-racist discussions at other universities, contributing their critical understanding. Transformative actions, such as these, illustrate the power of conscientização, developed through an anti-racist pedagogy, in driving students to become active citizens who recognize their capacity for leadership.[102]

Using Freire in Design Education

Freire's analysis of how our culture both constructs and is constructed by us, echoes the process of design. Willis draws upon Heidegger's concept of the hermeneutic circle, when she explains how "we design our world while our world acts back on us as designers".[103] Willis' statement not only acknowledges the pivotal role designers play in constructing the world but also highlights the importance of designers recognizing how they are then equally conditioned by their designs. Freire's critical dialogue can facilitate the critical awareness necessary for design students to recognize social inequalities and find innovative ways to disrupt this cycle: transforming society, rather than replicating complex issues of oppression.

However, Norman suggests that many design educators can lack the necessary critical awareness to fully engage with the complexity of social issues.[104] As Freire illuminates, well intentioned educators can equally be conditioned by the culture of silence until they do not see how the banking system approach dehumanizes.[105] Therefore, both teachers and students need to engage in critical dialogue around issues of social justice, especially those beyond the lived experience of the design educator. Without this dialogue, inequalities can easily be replicated through design education.[106] Sin et al. illustrate this through their example of design educators teaching students to assess the usability of a design. They point out how usability is often assessed through societies normative values; consequently, the ablest, racist, sexist and gender normative biases embedded in many designs, go unrecognized and unaddressed. This then further increases the digital marginalization of many social groups.[107] Therefore, Freire's pedagogy, which transforms the teacher/student relationship into one of mutual curiosity and dialectical knowledge production, provides a space where student and teacher can learn together, enabling both design students and design educators to engage with ideas beyond their own world view.

This critical dialogue is a direct threat to the banking system of education and works to transgress the neoliberal education of the elite.[108] Traditional design education often focuses on training, where students learn the processes required to work within the profession.[109] These processes are often taught through students responding to design briefs which invariably reflect the lived experience and learning context of the instructor.[110] Inequalities are then perpetuated, as students are only exposed to the limited lived experience of the design educator. This banking system approach to design education, also runs the risk of reinforcing the inequalities that exist within the design profession itself where "only certain kinds of design work are acknowledged, valorised, renumerated, and credited".[111] Freire's transformative pedagogy acts as a direct challenge to the banking system of education. By embracing a problem posing approach, both design educators and students can learn to question the societal norms that drive the process of design. Through critical dialogue with other students, clients and the wider community, design students can reveal the social inequalities that are perpetuated through design and work to find creative solutions. Once students recognize design as a process of praxis, they can work with others to initiate transformation.

Conclusion

Freire suggests that actively engaging in constructing and transforming the social world is our responsibility as active subjects.[112] However, complex systems of oppression condition people into passive beings, devoid of agency. Transformative pedagogy can expose the mechanisms of oppression; harnessing the power of education to transform not just the curriculum but also students' capacity to see their agency as active subjects, capable of transforming the world. For design students, whose primary purpose is to create, gaining a more critical awareness of the world is essential to prevent the replication of oppression. Design students can then utilize their creativity to devise innovative, equitable solutions to society's complex issues.

As Freire says,

> They had discovered not only that they could speak, but that their critical discourse upon the world, was a way of re-making that world.[113]

Notes

1 Paulo Freire, *The Politics of Education: Culture, Power and Liberation* (London: Bergin and Garvey, 1985), 12.
2 Paulo Freire, *Pedagogy of the Oppressed* (London: Penguin Books, 1970), 62.
3 Henry Giroux, "Rethinking Education as the Practice of Freedom: Paulo Freire and the Promise of Critical Pedagogy," *Policy Futures in Education* 8, no. 6 (2010): 716, https://doi.org/10.2304/pfie.2010.8.6.715.
4 Miguel Escobar, Alfredo L. Fernández, Gilberto Guevara-Niebla and Paulo Freire, *Paulo Freire on Higher Education: A Dialogue at the National University of Mexico* (Albany: State University of New York Press, 1994), 24–69; Freire, *Politics of Education*, 113–19; Peter Mayo, *Echoes from Freire for a Critically Engaged Pedagogy* (London: Bloomsbury Publishing, 2013), 36–44.
5 Paulo Freire, "A Response," in *Mentoring the Mentor: A Critical Dialogue with Paulo Freire*, ed. Paulo Freire, James W. Fraser, Donald Macedo, Tanya McKinnon, and William T. Stokes (New York: Peter Lang Publishing, 1997), 305.
6 Munif Nordin, "History and Epistemology of Universities," *Policy Ideas*, no. 41 (May 2017): 4–10; Sintayehu Kassaye Alemu, "The Meaning, Idea and History of University/Higher Education in Africa: A Brief Literature Review," *FIRE: Forum for International Research in Education* 4, no. 3 (2018): 211–14.
7 Giroux, *Rethinking Education*, 715.
8 Ibid; Rolf Straubhaar, Sascha Betts, and Sara Torres, "Pursuing Critical Consciousness on the Tenure Track: Towards a Humanizing Praxis within the Neoliberal University," in *Reinventing Pedagogy of the Oppressed: Contemporary Critical Perspectives*, ed. James D. Kirylo (London: Bloomsbury Academic, 2020), 191.

9 Mike Neary, "Teaching Excellence Framework: A Critical Response and an Alternative Future," *Journal of Contemporary European Research* 12, no. 3 (2016): 691.

10 Andrew Gunn, "Metrics and Methodologies for Measuring Teaching Quality in Higher Education: Developing the Teaching Excellence Framework (TEF)," *Educational Review* 70, no. 2 (January 2018): 129–48.

11 Office for Students, "Description of Student Outcome and Experience Measures Used in OfS Regulation: Definition of Measures and Methods Used to Construct and Present Them," (September 2022), https://www.officeforstudents.org.uk/media/6fec91a8-2826-4b15-9447-7e3de2dd7526/description-of-student-outcome-and-experience-measures.pdf

12 Giroux, *Rethinking Education*, 715.

13 Peter Mayo, *Gramsci, Freire and Adult Education: Possibilities for Transformative Action* (New York: Zed Books, 1999), 1.

14 Henry Giroux, "Introduction," in *The Politics of Education: Culture, Power and Liberation*, ed. Paulo Freire (London: Bergin and Garvey, 1985), xi–xxvi.

15 Paulo Freire and Donald Macedo, *Literacy: Reading the Word and the World* (London: Routledge, 1987), 122.

16 "Independent Panel Report to the Review of Post-18 Education and Funding," 2019, c.117, https://assets.publishing.service.gov.uk/government/uploads/system/uploads/attachment_data/file/805127/Review_of_post_18_education_and_funding.pdf

17 Department for Education, "Crackdown on Rip-off University Degrees," *Gov.UK Press Release*, July 17, 2023, https://www.gov.uk/government/news/crackdown-on-rip-off-university-degrees#:~:text=Students%20and%20taxpayers%20will%20be,and%20Education%20Secretary%20have%20announced.

18 Paulo Freire, *Pedagogy of the Heart* (New York: Bloomsbury, 1997), 98.

19 Murat Öztok, *The Hidden Curriculum of Online Learning: Understanding Social Justice through Critical Pedagogy* (Oxon: Routledge, 2020), 27–29.

20 Freire, *Pedagogy of Oppressed*, 17–19.

21 Ibid., 18.

22 Freire, *Politics of Education*, 71–75.

23 Paulo Freire, *Pedagogy in Process: The Letters to Guinea-Bissau*, trans. C. Hunter (London: Bloomsbury, 1978), 53.

24 Freire, *Pedagogy of Oppressed*, 159–75; Freire, *Politics of Education*, 71–75

25 Freire, *Pedagogy of Oppressed*, 33; Margaret Ledwith, *Community Development in Action* (Bristol: Policy Press, 2016), 86.

26 Freire, *Pedagogy of Oppressed*, 27.

27 Freire, *Politics of Education*, 30.

28 Ibid.

29 Paulo Freire, *Pedagogy of Freedom: Ethics, Democracy and Civic Courage*, trans. P. Clarke (Lanham, MD: Rowman and Littlefield Publishers, 1998), 25.

30 Paulo Freire, Maria Freire, and Walter de Oliveira, *Pedagogy of Solidarity* (Oxon: Routledge, 2014), 52.

31 Escobar et al., *Paulo Freire on Higher Education*, 31.

32 Ibid.

33 Freire, *Pedagogy of Freedom*, 26.

34 Freire, *Politics of Education*, 113.

35 Freire, *Pedagogy of Oppressed*, 54; Freire, *Politics of Education*.

36 Escobar et al., *Paulo Freire on Higher Education*, 58.

37 Freire, *Pedagogy of Oppressed*, 92–97; Paulo Freire, *Education for Critical Consciousness* (London: Continuum, 1974), 123–26; Freire, *Politics of Education*, 113–19; Paulo Freire, "A Response," in *Mentoring the Mentor: A Critical Dialogue with Paulo Freire*, ed. Paulo Freire, James W. Fraser, Donald Macedo, Tanya McKinnon, and William T. Stokes (New York: Peter Lang Publishing, 1997), 321

38 Escobar et al., *Paulo Freire on Higher Education*, 71–131; Freire, "A Response," 303–30.

39 Freire, "A Response," 309.

40 Catherine Bovill, "Student Engagement: Students as Active Partners in Shaping Their Learning Experience," *The Higher Education Academy*, November 1, 2010, https://www.advance-he.ac.uk/knowledge-hub/university-glasgow-students-and-staff-co-creating-curriculum; Samuel Severance, William R. Penuel, Tamara Sumner, and Heather Leary, "Organizing for Teacher Agency in Curricular Co-design," *Journal of the Learning Sciences* 25, no. 4 (2016): 531–64; Reza Ahmadi, "Student Voice, Culture, and Teacher Power in Curriculum Co-design within Higher Education: An Action-based Research Study," *International Journal for Academic Development* 28, no. 2 (2023): 177–89.

41 Freire, *Pedagogy of the Heart,* 47; Escobar et al., *Paulo Freire on Higher Education*, 33.

42 Freire, *Politics of Education*, 99, 100.

43 Paulo Freire, *Pedagogy of Hope: Reliving Pedagogy of the Oppressed*, trans. R. Barr (London: Bloomsbury Revelations, 1992), 30.

44 Mike Oliver, "Defining Impairment and Disability: Issues at Stake," in *Exploring the Divide: Illness and Disability*, ed. Colin Barnes and Geof Mercer (London: The Disability Press, 1996), 29–54; Sasha Costanza-Chock, *Design Justice: Community-Led Practices to Build the Worlds We Need* (London: MIT Press, 2020), 1–30.

45 Freire, *Pedagogy of Oppressed*, 27, 28; Freire, *Politics of Education*, 31.

46 Safiya Umoja Noble, *Algorithms of Oppression: How Search Engines Reinforce Racism* (New York: New York University Press, 2018), 2–6; Oliver, "Defining Impairment"; Costanza-Chock, *Design Justice,* 74; Azeezat Johnson and Remi Joseph-Salisbury, "'Are You Supposed to Be Here?' Racial Microaggressions and Knowledge Production in Higher Education," in *Dismantling Race in Higher Education: Racism, Whiteness and Decolonising the Academy*, ed. Jason Arday and Heidi Mirza (Palgrave Macmillan, 2018), 143–60.

47 Freire, *Pedagogy in Process*, 3.

48 Freire, *Politics of Education*, 69; Freire, *Pedagogy of Oppressed*, 31, 32.

49 Freire, *Pedagogy of Oppressed,* 32, 33.

50 Ibid., 2.

51 Ibid.
52 Ibid., 52–67
53 Stephen Ball, "Performativities and Fabrications in the Education Economy: Towards the Performative Society?" *Australian Educational Research* 27, no. 2 (2000).
54 Freire, *Pedagogy of Oppressed*; Freire, *Education for Critical Consciousness*; Freire, *Mentoring the Mentor*, 303–30.
55 Freire, *Education for Critical Consciousness*, 107.
56 Amsler, *Radical Democracy*, 8.
57 Design Justice Network, "Home," accessed June 3 2023, https://designjustice.org/; Yanatan Miller, "Tech Won't Build It," *Humanity in Action*, 2021, https://humanityinaction.org/action_project/landecker-democracy-fellowship-tech-wont-build-it/.
58 Costanza-Chock, *Design Justice*, 1–5.
59 Noble, *Algorithms of Oppression*, 1–6.
60 Freire, *Pedagogy in Process*, 18.
61 Freire, "A Response."
62 Freire, *Pedagogy of Oppressed*, 31.
63 Ibid., 48.
64 Freire, *Pedagogy of Oppressed*, 90, 91; Freire, *Politics of Education*, 87–91.
65 Freire, *Pedagogy of Oppressed*, 106–64; Freire, *Politics of Education*, 167–73.
66 bell hooks, *Teaching to Transgress* (Oxon: Routledge, 1994), 12.
67 Freire, *Politics of Education*, 12.
68 Freire, *Mentoring the Mentor*.
69 Freire, *Politics of Education*, 1–4.
70 Ibid., 12.
71 Roddy Slorach, *A Very Capitalist Condition: A History and Politics of Disability* (London: Bookmarks Publications, 2016), chap. 12, Kindle.
72 Charlotte Clark, "Classification and Stigma: Theorising the Identity Impact of Dyslexia for Students in UK Higher Education" (PhD thesis, UCL Discovery, 2022), 205 https://discovery.ucl.ac.uk/id/eprint/10156218/2/PostViva%20thesis%20FINAL%20LIBRARY%20COPY%20CHHC%20Sep22%20pdf.pdf
73 Freire, *Education for Critical Consciousness*, 21.
74 Andre Delbecq and Andrew Van de Ven, "A Group Process Model for Problem Identification and Program Planning," *The Journal of Applied Behavioral Science* 7, no. 4 (1971): 466–92.
75 Graeme Paton, "Ofsted: English Standards in Primary School 'Too Low'," *The Telegraph*, March 15, 2012, https://www.telegraph.co.uk/education/educationnews/9144266/Ofsted-English-standards-in-primary-schools-too-low.html; "Figures Show Drop in Scottish Literacy Pupil Rates," *BBC News*, May 9, 2017, https://www.bbc.co.uk/news/uk-scotland-scotland-politics-39856284
76 Jennifer Buckingham, "Low Literacy Cannot be Tolerated or Excused Any Longer," *ABC News*, March 22, 2016, https://www.abc.net.au/news/2016-03-22/buckingham-low-literacy-cannot-be-tolerated/7266410
77 David Vincent, "Reading and Writing," in *The History of Reading*, ed. Shafquat Towheed, Rosalind Crone, and Katie Halsey (Oxon: Routledge, 2011), 161–70.

78 Robert Darnton, "First Steps Towards a History of Reading," in *The History of Reading*, ed. Shafquat Towheed, Rosalind Crone, and Katie Halsey (Oxon: Routledge, 2011), 23–35; Vincent, "Reading and Writing," 161–70.

79 Henry Giroux, "Preface," in *Literacy: Reading the Word and the World*, ed. Paulo Freire and Donald Macedo (London: Routledge, 1987), 1–19.

80 Freire, *Politics of Education*, 1; Margaret Meek, "Forward," in *Literacy: Reading the Word and the World*, ed. Paulo Freire and Donald Macedo (London: Routledge, 1987), vii–x.

81 Margaret Meek, *How Text Teach What Readers Learn* (Gloustershire: The Thimble Press, 1988), 8; Jane Perryman, Stephen Ball, Meg Maguire, and Annette Braun, "Life in the Pressure Cooker – School League Tables and English and Mathematics Teachers' Responses to Accountability in a Results-Driven Era," *British Journal of Educational Studies* 59, no. 2 (June 2011): 179–95.

82 Craig Collinson, " 'Lexism' and the Temporal Problem of Defining 'Dyslexia'," in *Changing Social Attitudes Towards Disability: Perspectives from Historical, Cultural and Educational Studies*, ed. David Bolt (London: Routledge, 2014), 153–61.

83 Judith Fettley, "On the Politics of Literacy," in *The History of Reading*, ed. Shafquat Towheed, Rosalind Crone, and Katie Halsey (Oxon: Routledge, 2011), 93.

84 Freire, *Pedagogy of Oppressed*, 47, 48.

85 Beth Sennett, "Unveiling the World: Critical Dialogue and the Process of Conscientization with Dyslexic Students in Higher Education" (EdD thesis, University of Winchester, 2020), 71, https://winchester.elsevier-pure.com/en/studentTheses/unveiling-the-world.

86 Freire, *Politics of Education*, 71–77.

87 Sennett, "Unveiling the World," 67.

88 Freire, *Pedagogy of Oppressed*, 17.

89 Ivan Illich, *Deschooling Society* (London: Marion Boyars, 1970).

90 Sennett, "Unveiling the World," 82.

91 Ibid., 84.

92 Ibid., 119.

93 Ibid., 136.

94 Ibid., 111.

95 hooks, *Teaching to Transgress*, 144.

96 Freire, *Pedagogy of Oppressed*, 33; Freire, *Politics of Education*, 76.

97 hooks, *Teaching to Transgress*, 140; Beverly Tatum, *Can We Talk about Race? And Other Conversations in an Era of School Resegregation* (Bolston: Beacon Press, 2008), 124–29.

98 Ngũgĩ wa Thiong'o, *Decolonising the Mind: The Politics of Language in African Literature* (London: East African Educational Publishers, 1992), 16.

99 Tatum, *Can We Talk about Race?* 35.

100 Brian Arao and Kristi Clemens, "A New Way to Frame Dialogue around Diversity and Social Justice," in *The Art of Effective Facilitation: Reflections from Social Justice Educators*, ed. Lisa M. Landreman (Virginia: Stylus Publishing, 2013).

101 Freire, *Pedagogy of Oppressed*, 53.

102 Tatum, *Can We Talk about Race?* 30–31; hooks, *Teaching to Transgress*, 14.
103 Anne-Marie Willis, "Ontological Designing," *Design Philosophy Papers* 4, no. 2 (2006): 69–92.
104 Don Norman, "Why Design Education Must Change," *Columns (blog)*, Core77, November 26, 2010, https://www.core77.com/posts/17993/why-design-education-must-change-17993.
105 Freire, *Pedagogy of Oppressed*, 56.
106 Costanza-Chock, *Design Justice,* 83, 84.
107 Jaisie Sin, Cosmin Munteanu, Michael Nixon, Velian Pandeliev, Garreth W. Tigwell, Kristen Shinohara, Anthony Tang, and Steve Szigeti, "Uncovering Inclusivity Gaps in Design Pedagogy Through the Digital Design Marginalization Framework," *Frontiers in Computer Science* 4 (2022): 04–08.
108 Freire, *Pedagogy of Oppressed*, 55.
109 Aidan Rowe, "Participatory Action Research and Design Pedagogy: Perspectives for Design Education," *Art, Design & Communication in Higher Education* 19, no. 1 (2020): 54.
110 Ibid.
111 Costanza-Chock, *Design Justice*, 14.
112 Freire, *Pedagogy of Freedom*, 25.
113 Freire, *Pedagogy of Hope*, 31.

Bibliography

Ahmadi, Reza. "Student Voice, Culture, and Teacher Power in Curriculum Co-design within Higher Education: An Action-based Research Study." *International Journal for Academic Development* 28, no. 2 (2023): 177–89.
Alemu, Sintayehu Kassaye. "The Meaning, Idea and History of University/Higher Education in Africa: A Brief Literature Review." *FIRE: Forum for International Research in Education* 4, no. 3 (2018).
Amsler, Sarah. *The Education of Radical Democracy*. Oxon: Routledge, 2015.
Arao, Brian, and Kristi Clemens, "A New Way to Frame Dialogue Around Diversity and Social Justice." In *The Art of Effective Facilitation: Reflections from Social Justice Educators*, edited by Lisa M. Landreman. Virginia: Stylus Publishing, 2013.
Ball, Stephen. "Performativities and Fabrications in the Education Economy: Towards the Performative Society?" *Australian Educational Research* 27, no 2 (2000). https://link.springer.com/article/10.1007/BF03219719
Bovill, Catherine. "Student Engagement: Students as Active Partners in Shaping Their Learning Experience." *The Higher Education Academy*, November 1, 2010. https://www.advance-he.ac.uk/knowledge-hub/university-glasgow-students-and-staff-co-creating-curriculum
Clark, Charlotte. "Classification and Stigma: Theorising the Identity Impact of Dyslexia for Students in UK Higher Education." PhD thesis, UCL Discovery, 2022, 205. https://discovery.ucl.ac.uk/id/eprint/10156218/2/PostViva%20thesis%20FINAL%20LIBRARY%20COPY%20CHHC%20Sep22%20pdf.pdf

Collinson, Craig. " 'Lexism' and the Temporal Problem of Defining 'Dyslexia'." In *Changing Social Attitudes towards Disability: Perspectives from Historical, Cultural and Educational Studies*, edited by David Bolt, 153–61. London: Routledge, 2014.

Costanza-Chock, Sasha. *Design Justice: Community-Led Practices to Build the Worlds We Need*. London: MIT Press, 2020.

Darnton, Robert. "First Steps Towards a History of Reading." In *The History of Reading*, edited by Shafquat Towheed, Rosalind Crone, and Katie Halsey, 23–35. Oxon: Routledge, 2011.

Delbecq, Andre L., and Andrew H. Van de Ven. "A Group Process Model for Problem Identification and Program Planning." *The Journal of Applied Behavioral Science* 7, no. 4 (1971): 466–92.

Department for Education. "Crackdown on Rip-off University Degrees." *Gov. UK Press Release*, July 17, 2023. https://www.gov.uk/government/news/crackdown-on-rip-off-university-degrees#:~:text=Students%20and%20taxpayers%20will%20be,and%20Education%20Secretary%20have%20announced, accessed July 23, 2023.

Design Justice Network. "Home." Accessed June 3, 2023. https://designjustice.org/

Escobar, Miguel, Alfredo L. Fernández, Gilberto Guevara-Niebla, and Paulo Freire. *Paulo Freire on Higher Education: A Dialogue at the National University of Mexico*. Albany: State University of New York Press, 1994.

Fettley, Judith. "On the Politics of Literacy." In *The History of Reading*, edited by Shafquat Towheed, Rosalind Crone, and Katie Halsey, 93–98. Oxon: Routledge, 2011.

Freire, Paulo. *Education for Critical Consciousness*. London: Continuum, 1974.
———. *Pedagogy of Freedom: Ethics, Democracy and Civic Courage*. Translated by P. Clarke. Lanham, MD: Rowman and Littlefield Publishers, 1998.
———. *Pedagogy of the Heart*. New York: Bloomsbury, 1997.
———. *Pedagogy of Hope: Reliving Pedagogy of the Oppressed*. Translated by R. Barr. London: Bloomsbury Revelations, 1992.
———. *Pedagogy of the Oppressed*. London: Penguin Books, 1970.
———. *Pedagogy in Process: The Letters to Guinea-Bissau*. Translated by C. Hunter. London: Bloomsbury, 1978.
———. *The Politics of Education: Culture, Power and Liberation*. London: Bergin and Garvey, 1985.
———. "A Response." In *Mentoring the Mentor: A Critical Dialogue with Paulo Freire*, edited by Paulo Freire, Paulo, James W. Fraser, Donald Macedo, Tanya McKinnon, and William T. Stokes, 303–30. New York: Peter Lang Publishing, 1997.

Freire, Paulo, and Donald Macedo. *Literacy: Reading the Word and the World*. London: Routledge, 1987.

Freire, Paulo, Freire Maria, and de Oliveira Walter. *Pedagogy of Solidarity*. Oxon: Routledge, 2014.

Giroux, Henry. "Introduction." In *The Politics of Education: Culture, Power and Liberation,* edited by Paulo Freire. London: Bergin and Garvey, 1985.
———. "Preface." In *Literacy: Reading the Word and the World*, edited by Paulo Freire and Donald Macedo. London: Routledge, 1987.

———. "Rethinking Education as the Practice of Freedom: Paulo Freire and the Promise of Critical Pedagogy." *Policy Futures in Education* 8, no. 6 (2010). https://doi.org/10.2304/pfie.2010.8.6.715.

Gunn, Andrew. "Metrics and Methodologies for Measuring Teaching Quality in Higher Education: Developing the Teaching Excellence Framework (TEF)." *Educational Review* 70, no. 2 (January 2018): 129–48.

hooks, bell. *Teaching to Transgress*. Oxon: Routledge, 1994.

Illich, Ivan. *Deschooling Society*. London: Marion Boyars, 1970.

"Independent Panel Report to the Review of Post-18 Education and Funding." 2019, c.117. https://assets.publishing.service.gov.uk/government/uploads/system/uploads/attachment_data/file/805127/Review_of_post_18_education_and_funding.pdf

Ledwith, Margaret. *Community Development in Action*. Bristol: Policy Press, 2016.

Mayo, Peter. *Echoes from Freire for a Critically Engaged Pedagogy*. London: Bloomsbury Publishing, 2013.

———. *Gramsci, Freire and Adult Education: Possibilities for Transformative Action*. New York: Zed Books, 1999.

Miller, Yanatan. "Tech Won't Build It." *Humanity in Action*, 2021. https://humanityinaction.org/action_project/landecker-democracy-fellowship-tech-wont-build-it/.

Neary, Mike. "Teaching Excellence Framework: A Critical Response and an Alternative Future." *Journal of Contemporary European Research* 12, no. 3 (2016). https://www.jcer.net/index.php/jcer/article/view/779/591

Noble, Safiya Umoja. *Algorithms of Oppression: How Search Engines Reinforce Racism*. New York: New York University Press, 2018.

Nordin, Munif. "History and Epistemology of Universities." *Policy Ideas*, no. 41 (2017). https://www.researchgate.net/publication/318360442_History_and_Epistemology_of_Universities?enrichId=rgreq-05c5e28b55a997357b-6c609a8b431f33-XXX&enrichSource=Y292ZXJQYWdlOzMxODM2MDQ0MjtBUzo1MTUxNDI4MjUxOTc1NjhAMTQ5OTgzMTAyODg0N g%3D%3D&el=1_x_2&_esc=publicationCoverPdf

Norman, Don. "Why Design Education Must Change." *Columns (blog)*, Core77, November 26, 2010. https://www.core77.com/posts/17993/why-design-education-must-change-17993.

Office for Students. "Description of Student Outcome and Experience Measures Used in OfS Regulation: Definition of Measures and Methods Used to Construct and Present Them." September 2022. https://www.officeforstudents.org.uk/media/6fec91a8-2826-4b15-9447-7e3de2dd7526/description-of-student-outcome-and-experience-measures.pdf

Oliver, Mike. "Defining Impairment and Disability: Issues at Stake." In *Exploring the Divide: Illness and Disability,* edited by Colin Barnes and Geof Mercer. London: The Disability Press, 1996.

Öztok, Murat. *The Hidden Curriculum of Online Learning: Understanding Social Justice through Critical Pedagogy*. Oxon: Routledge, 2020.

Rowe, Aidan. "Participatory Action Research and Design Pedagogy: Perspectives for Design Education." *Art, Design & Communication in Higher Education* 19, no. 1 (2020): 52–64.

Sennett, Beth. "Unveiling the World: Critical Dialogue and the Process of Conscientization with Dyslexic Students in Higher Education." EdD thesis, University of Winchester, 2020. https://winchester.elsevierpure.com/en/studentTheses/unveiling-the-world.

Severance, Samuel, William R. Penuel, Tamara Sumner, and Heather Leary. "Organizing for Teacher Agency in Curricular Co-design." *Journal of the Learning Sciences* 25, no. 4 (2016): 531–64.

Sin, Jaisie, Cosmin Munteanu, Michael Nixon, Velian Pandeliev, Garreth W. Tigwell, Kristen Shinohara, Anthony Tang, and Steve Szigeti. "Uncovering Inclusivity Gaps in Design Pedagogy Through the Digital Design Marginalization Framework." *Frontiers in Computer Science* 4 (2022): 01–11.

Straubhaar, Rolf, Sascha Betts, and Sara Torres. "Pursuing Critical Consciousness on the Tenure Track: Towards a Humanizing Praxis within the Neoliberal University." In *Reinventing Pedagogy of the Oppressed: Contemporary Critical Perspectives*, edited by James D. Kirylo, 191–200. London: Bloomsbury Academic, 2020.

Tatum, Beverly. *Can We Talk about Race? And Other Conversations in an Era of School Resegregation*. Bolston: Beacon Press, 2007.

Vincent, David. "Reading and Writing." In *The History of Reading*, edited by Shafquat Towheed, Rosalind Crone, and Katie Halsey, 161–70. Oxon: Routledge, 2011.

wa Thiong'o, Ngũgĩ. *Decolonising the Mind: The Politics of Language in African Literature*. London: East African Educational Publishers, 1992.

Willis, Anne-Marie. "Ontological Designing." *Design Philosophy Papers* 4, no. 2 (2006).

2 Transformative Teaching

New Roles of Experiential Design Educators in the Post-Covid Era

Juanjuan "June" He

Introduction

In 2021, during the Covid-19 pandemic, I changed my career path from a professional designer working in the industry to an assistant professor guiding college students in navigating between academia and the real world. There were unprecedented challenges. Students were back from the lockdown after eighteen months. They were unfamiliar with social life and the communities around them. Based on this reality, I began to develop pedagogical innovations that could bring them together and collaborate with the communities beyond the campus. The goal is to create opportunities for them to form trust and support in a new learning experience, and to co-design with the community's needs in mind. This chapter explores my experimental course *Aging & Design* at Drexel University in the Spring term of 2022. It introduces the pedagogical framework to achieve students' transformative learning outcomes. In addition, it reflects on the new role of an experiential design educator in this post-pandemic era.

Transformative Learning

Constructivism, initiated by the Swiss developmental psychologist Jean Piaget, believed that learning is experience-based, and knowledge is constructed by the learner's experience.[1] Soviet psychologist Lev Vygotsky stated that social interaction plays a major role in contributing to the learning experience.[2] Vygotsky further emphasized that language and culture are essential in developing human intelligence and perception of the world; therefore, knowledge is co-constructed by interacting with other people in a social setting.[3] Figure 2.1 illustrates Vygotsky's social constructivism theory. Based on Vygotsky's social constructivism theory, I utilized the socialization component in the course design. Small teams were formed in the classroom. Each team was comprised of one older participant from the local immigrant community, two interdisciplinary students and one volunteer interpreter. During the term, they collaborated with each other, provided with guided course instructions and materials to acquire knowledge and create innovative solutions.

DOI: 10.4324/9781032705927-3

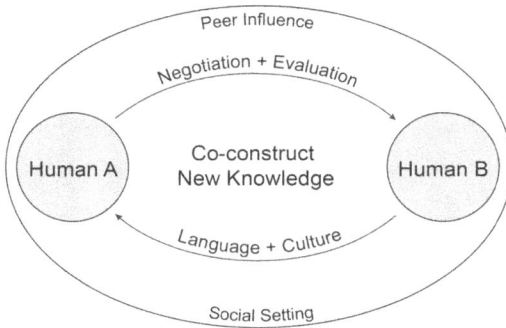

Figure 2.1 Vygotsky's social constructivism theory. Diagram by the author

As described by American sociologist Jack Mezirow, transformative learning is "an orientation which holds that the way learners interpret and reinterpret their sense experience is central to making meaning and hence learning".[4] Transformative learning theory is in essence constructivism. It's learning by experiencing the process. My course pedagogy is based on transformative learning theory. Instead of delivering knowledge to students directly, I taught them the methods and the tools, guided them in interacting with the community members, assigned them reflective writings and discussions at various stages and helped them iterate on their design prototypes. The students gained their insights by actively exploring, experimenting, collaborating, analyzing and reflecting. In this way, students were more receptive to the newly gained knowledge and tend to have a stronger grasp of it. Figure 2.2 is a diagram to represent the application of transformative learning theory and constructivism theory in the *Aging & Design* class during the Spring 2022 term at Drexel University.

Empathic Design

"Empathy is our ability to see the world through other people's eyes – to see what they see, feel what they feel and experience things as they do".[5] "Empathic design is an approach that relies on the user being an active partner within the information creation process. Developing empathy enables the designer to become closer to the partner using respectful curiosity, genuine understanding, and suspension of judgment".[6] It is imperative for designers to use empathy to understand the target users' true needs before creating any tangible solutions.

In the *Aging & Design* course, empathy was introduced early on before students' workshops with older immigrant participants. Assumptions did not

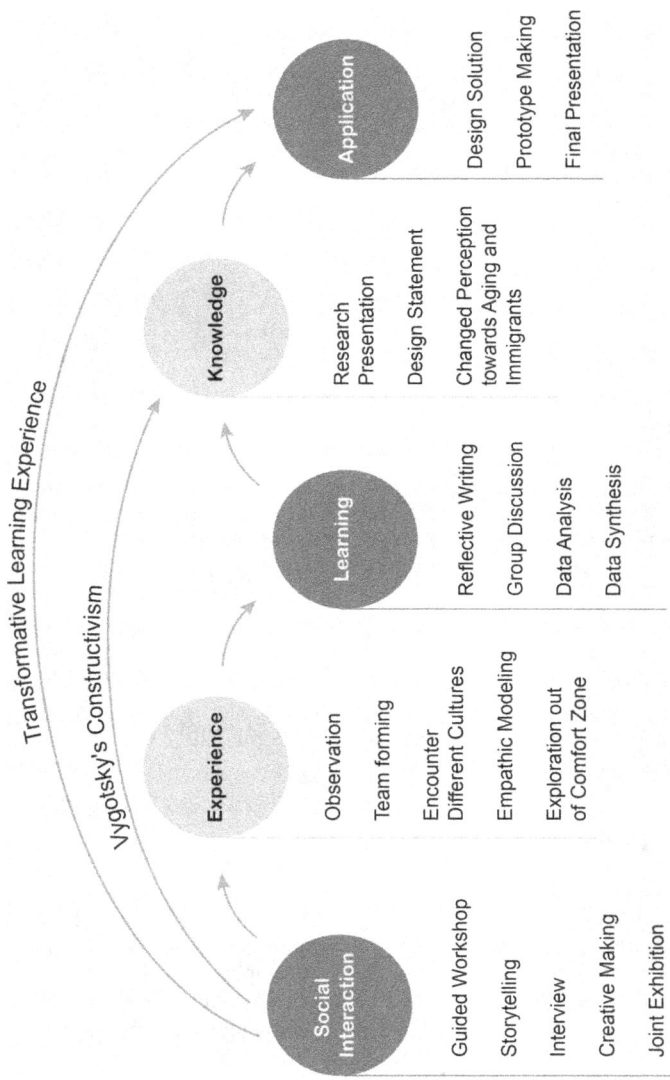

Figure 2.2 Transformative learning theory and constructivism theory in the *Aging & Design* class, Spring 2022 term. Diagram by the author

work here. Instead of traditional "design for" the users, students were guided to "design with" the users. Every decision they made should be based on the feedback they received from the older participants, especially when the students did not know these immigrant users' cultures, languages, and values beforehand. Empathic design plays a critical role here as we embrace human-centered design methodologies.

Community-Based Participatory Design

Empathic design is one way to achieve human-centered design, but it's not enough. How might we balance the power dynamics in the intergenerational team? How do we know that the designers are not misrepresenting the needs of the older users? Equity-centered design methods are another area we emphasized in the educational process. In this *Aging & Design* course, the community-based participatory design framework was introduced at the beginning of the term. "Participatory Design works to involve all stakeholders (e.g., customers, employees, partners, citizens, consumers, etc.) in the design process as a means to better understand user needs".[7] Community-based participatory design expands the stakeholders to community leaders and members, engaging them in the design process, including their specific needs through their unique cultural context. Figure 2.3 shows the design methodologies I taught students in this course.

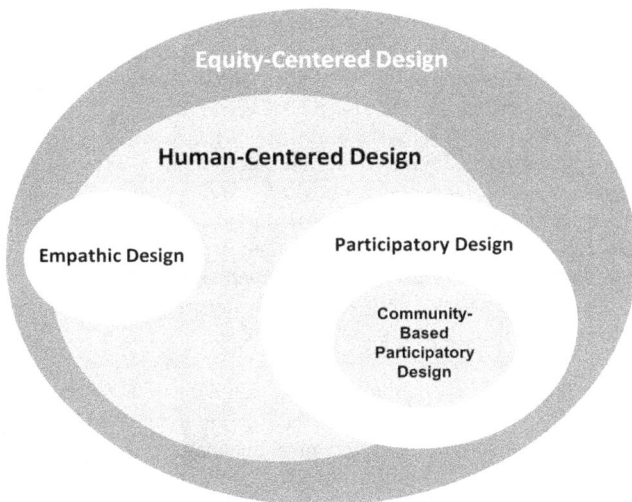

Equity-Centered Design

Human-Centered Design

Empathic Design

Participatory Design

Community-Based Participatory Design

Figure 2.3 Design methodologies used in this class. Diagram by the author

Equity-Centered Design

Equity-centered design methodologies are inclusive, participatory and empathic. They focus on the designer, as well as the users to recognize their own "identity, values, emotions, biases, assumptions and situatedness" before going to the design practice.[8] Equity-centered community design (ECCD) is "a unique creative problem-solving process based on equity, humility-building, integrating history and healing practices, addressing power dynamics, and co-creating with the community".[9]

Older immigrant adults' cultures and voices are often neglected in the mainstream media. During the pandemic, hate crimes and discrimination towards older Asians increased dramatically. Addressing these issues by conducting secondary research and primary research with the older adults, students increased their awareness of the situation those older participants are in, broke the stereotype of older people and immigrants, and recognized their own implicit bias, thus transforming their perceptions towards aging and design, and became equity-centered designers.

An Experiential Design Educator

What is the role of a design educator in the classroom? Different educators might have different answers. Lecture, seminar, and studio classes all share distinctive features and learning styles, which require educators to play different roles respectively. To facilitate transformative learning, we will first investigate experiential learning theory and therefore understand how to be an experiential design educator in the current world.

American educational theorist, David A. Kolb, described the characteristics of experiential learning in his book *Experiential Learning: Experience As The Source Of Learning And Development*:

1. *Learning is best conceived as a process, not in terms of outcomes.*
2. *Learning is a continuous process grounded in experience.*
3. *The process of learning requires the resolution of conflicts between dialectically opposed modes of adaptation to the world.*
4. *Learning is a holistic process of adaptation to the world.*
5. *Learning involves transactions between the person and the environment.*
6. *Learning is the process of creating knowledge.*[10]

Kolb's principles of experiential learning echo the transformative learning theory from Mezirow, with both centering on the interactive experience between the human and the environment as the continuous learning process, thus creating knowledge. As design educators, how can we create this unique environment to encourage learning? How can we conquer the constantly emerging barriers in the process? How can we guide the students in the right direction to gain new knowledge? Based on my experiment, I would like to introduce you to three roles of the design educator: design facilitator, design acupuncturist and design therapist.

Design Facilitator

As a design educator, the first role I played in the course pedagogy develop-ment was design facilitator. Bringing students to engage with the local older immigrant community was a crucial component of the course. I initiated com-munity outreach and networking half a year before launching the course to make sure the learning experience is holistic and multidimensional as trans-formative learning requires an engaging experience for all participants. The main task here was working with university resources to enroll interdiscipli-nary students across the campus as well as partnering with community non-profit organizations to reach out to older community members from a variety of cultural backgrounds. Due to the diverse languages involved among the students and local participants, it was vital to recruit volunteer interpreters and translators from surrounding communities to assist in conversations during the course. All these tasks were completed before the first day of the class. At this point, the educator functioned as a design facilitator to collect and organ-ize all the resources to make sure the course design is comprehensive and supported beyond the classroom, ultimately creating a positive experience for each participant involved in this course moving forward.

One example of the design facilitator's role was to invite older partici-pants to the course. How did we do this? We had the students enrolled in the class by the university, but we needed to invite the older participants. First, virtual conferences were hosted with leaders from local non-profit organi-zations, where we pitched our proposal, answered questions and discussed the next step. Then, interested non-profit leaders distributed the multi-lingual course flyers to the older adults in the community to sign up. During this time, the design facilitator hosted several virtual meetings to give a safe space for potential older participants to ask questions before they decide to partici-pate. Meanwhile, the social workers at the non-profit organizations worked together with the design facilitator to reach out to individual older adults who did not know how to use the virtual platforms. With both online and offline approaches and support from the local leaders and social workers, eventually, we enrolled enough older participants to form teams with students. After the course started, the design facilitator formed a group on social media with all the older adults to continuously answer questions and remind them of event dates throughout the term. This contributed to building the transformative learning experience in the class by facilitating communication and interaction channels between the two distinctively different groups of learners.

Another example of the design facilitator's role is to match team mem-bers, including students, older adults, and volunteer interpreters. Before the term started, the design facilitator reached out to each enrolled student to understand their majors and cultural backgrounds. When matching the students to form small teams, the design facilitator made sure students in each team were from different majors and cultural backgrounds so they could learn from each other in an inclusive manner. At the same time, the design facilitator communicated with older adults to know their cultural backgrounds and particular needs. It would be great if some students shared the same language with certain older adults. In that case, they were matched together in a team. Otherwise, the teams would require the design facilitator to look for volunteer interpreters to help the communication flow, including designing flyers and distributing flyers to other community partners and university programs. Oftentimes, we would receive volunteers from university students, community members, family, and friends from older participants.

Design Acupuncturist

Acupuncture is a traditional Chinese healing method. It uses thin metal needles to penetrate acupoints in the human body to release pain and improve health. It works in the nerve cells and systems of the human body.[11] Each acupoint focuses on one nerve system of the body, by manipulating the needles with specific movements from a trained acupuncturist, the symptom of the illness could be relieved. According to the theory from traditional Chinese medicine, the human body has more than 2,000 acupoints connected by pathways. They create an energy flow through the body that maintains overall health. Blockage of the energy flow can cause illness. Applying adjustments to acupoints could improve energy flow and health.[12]

Horst Rittel, a design theorist and university professor of design methodology in Germany, popularized the concept of *Wicked Problems* in the 1960s, stating that most design problems are wicked problems.[13] According to Rittel, wicked problems refer to complex and ambiguous issues that are often difficult to define, have multiple stakeholders with conflicting perspectives and do not have clear-cut solutions.[14] To solve wicked problems, traditional linear approaches are inadequate. Instead, we must embrace a more collaborative, iterative and adaptive approach because we are facing an ecosystem here, not a single problem.

In essence, designing the course *Aging & Design* with a variety of stakeholders and unforeseeable issues was itself a wicked problem. Each wicked problem is like a web, with interlacing problems weaving into each other and hard to navigate using the traditional linear mindset. It's like acupoints in the human body. Figure 2.4 and Figure 2.5 are two diagrams demonstrating wicked problems and communication flow relevant to designing this course compared to the map of human acupoints and energy flow.

The human body's every acupoint is like each stakeholder in the course design process. To make sure the communication flows smoothly among different stakeholders, the instructor needs to negotiate and listen to the needs and voices of each of them. Similarly, to enhance the positive energy flow along the

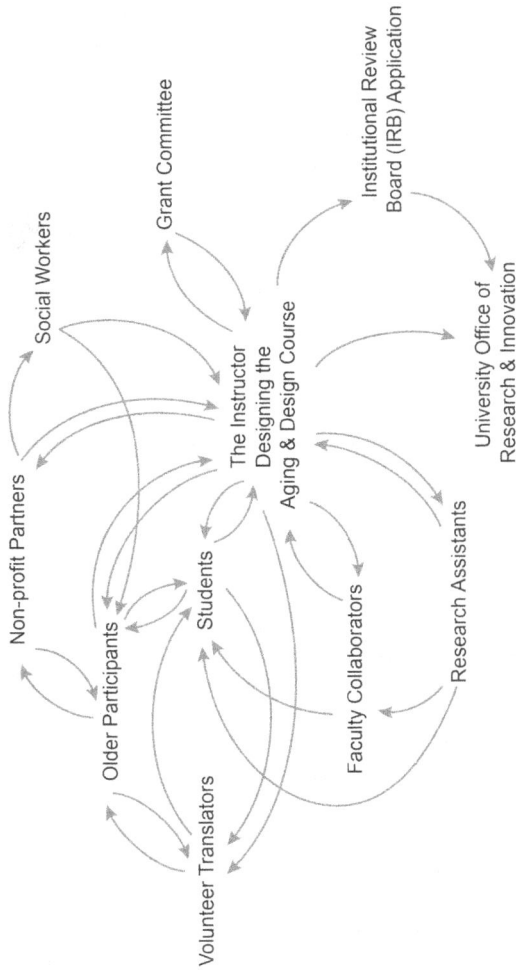

Figure 2.4 A diagram illustrates the complexity of the wicked problem of designing a community-based co-design course. The arrows represent communication flow among various groups or organizations. Created by the author

Human body meridians

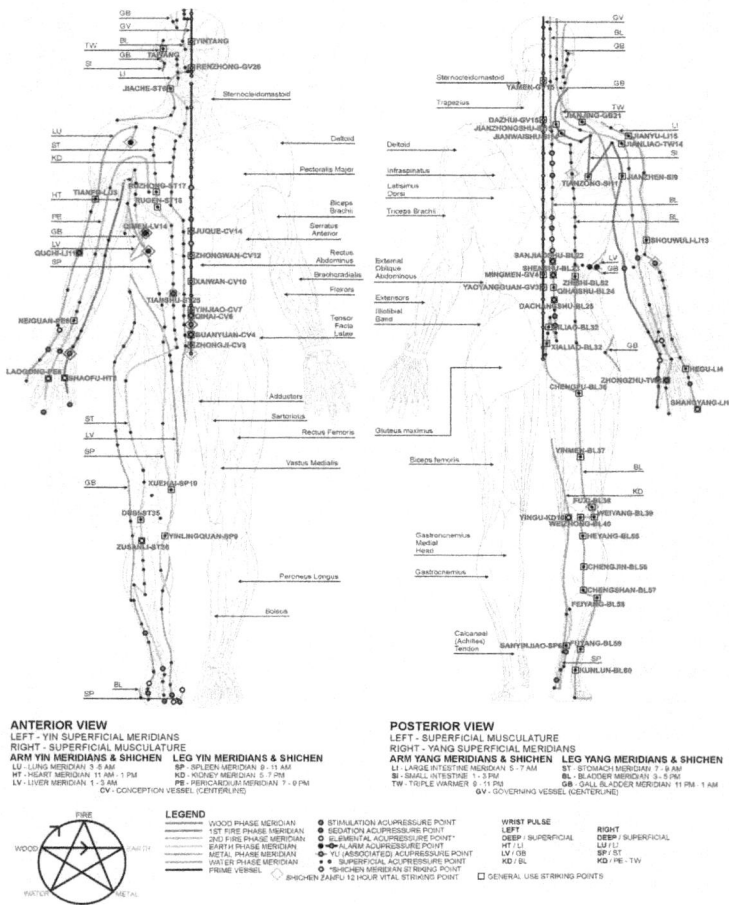

Figure 2.5 Map of human body meridians and acupoints.[15] From Wikimedia Commons

meridians in the human body, an acupuncturist uses special needles to stimulate the relevant acupoints, thus making sure there is no blockage along the way.

As a design educator, to successfully guide the flow of the course and tackle this wicked problem, I acted as a design acupuncturist to pinpoint the barriers in the process to resolve the overall disruption. For instance, some community participants were comfortable with in-person workshops while others were not due to the Covid-19 situation. How can we make sure they have equal opportunities to participate in our activities? Hence, the design acupuncturist must figure out a solution to cater to different needs. Knowing the exact pain point on the web, I designed methods for in-person and virtual meetings and adjusted the workshop timeline accordingly. Not all the community participants were confident technology users, so we employed various software to ease the process and increase in-person interaction. For example, students visited participants' homes and delivered toolkits before the virtual workshop took place. By removing these barriers, we revived the energy flow of the course, thus enhancing communication among team members. Another example was guiding the students to communicate with older adults outside the classroom. The pain point here was the language. Students and older adults need interpreters to create the bridge for dialogue, so efficiently coordinating timing with everyone became critical for the success of the project.

By adjusting methods and creating solutions at various points and pathways of the course flow, the educator as the design acupuncturist solves the wicked problems in a systematic way, making sure to bring an enriching learning experience for students, community participants and everyone else involved.

Design Therapist

A design acupuncturist focuses on the physical side of the course flow, including the structure, method, timeline, location and assignment, while a design therapist pays attention to the emotional side of the course design, like students' fulfillment, challenges, collaboration and communication. A design educator needs to take care of both the physical side of the course as well as the emotional side. One-on-one meetings with students, feedback discussions with community participants, follow-up sessions with volunteers and check-in with partner organizations and collaborators, all contribute to the well-being of the course and the people involved. Because of the language and cultural differences between the students and older adults, the design therapist's role is critical to help navigate the direction of the collaboration.

The older adults who participated in our course used to go to the community center in Philadelphia regularly to join group events before the pandemic. However, because of Covid-19, the community center was closed. Some older participants expressed loneliness due to isolation at home for a long time. Through storytelling and interviews, students understood their needs. Groups of students planned to go to visit their paired older adults' homes after the class and to deliver co-create toolkits. However, because of language differences and the schedule of the volunteer, one group of students called me while they were at the entrance of the apartment building of an older adult. As a design therapist, I helped translate and connect the students and the older adult through the phone to make sure their visit was meaningful and effective. During the visit, the older adult prepared food for the students, gave them a tour of her apartment and shared her fascinating artwork with them. Students had a great experience, as well as the older adult. Later the older adult wrote in her reflection: "I've never been happier like today. Since quarantine, I stayed home most of the time and don't have any social life".

Design therapist is different from art therapist. An art therapist is a mental health professional who uses the creative process of making art and applied psychological theory to help clients heal.[16] A design therapist protects the mental health of all the stakeholders involved in the design process to achieve the final goal of creating an innovative co-created solution. In the course experience, some effects of art therapy were achieved as a by-product of our activities, like co-creating guided artwork. But the goal here was not to heal our participants through art making but to understand them better as human beings, their values, emotions, fears and desires. A design therapist safeguards the emotional journey of each team member. The qualitative data collected through the course reflects that students, older participants and interpreters gained positive emotional changes through this course. In fact, a design therapist's role is not only needed in this experimental design course, but in a typical multidisciplinary design team in the industry as well.

Pedagogical Innovation

In the process of developing this course, my goal was to create an experiential learning experience for students and community participants by exposing them to cross-cultural communication and empathic design activities despite language barriers. During the Spring term of 2022, interdisciplinary college students from Drexel University were paired with older Asian adults in the communities of Philadelphia in the *Aging & Design* course. The students were from diverse backgrounds, including undergraduate, graduate students and international students. Their majors cover product design, biomedical engineering, urban strategy, economics, marketing, interior design, health sciences and more. Older participants were from two non-profit organizations: Philadelphia Senior Center and SEAMAAC (Southeast Asian Mutual Assistance Associations Coalition). They were over sixty years old, and all immigrants from East Asia and South Asia, speaking Mandarin or Cantonese. Most of them could not communicate using English. Thirteen students and seven older adults participated in this collaborative course.

Another significant reason to develop this course was to help voice the needs of an aging society and build Stop Asian Hate initiatives. Before the workshops, I hosted Zoom meetings to talk to older adults about their concerns and answer their questions. Many expressed their worries about discrimination and hate crimes towards Asians during the Covid-19 pandemic, especially older people who do not speak English. This course gives tools to students and older adults to break down stereotypes by creating individual relationships. Exploratory activities were introduced to the course pedagogy, including empathic modeling, storytelling, co-create and co-design workshops, home-visiting and public-facing co-exhibition.

Empathic Design Research

Empathic design research uses a research process based on the collaboration of both users and designers to identify authentic human needs instead of assumed needs.[17] At the beginning of the course, students were introduced to the theory and tools of empathic design to help them prepare for the incoming workshop with older community members. Young students tend to use problem-solving skills based on their own perspectives and experiences. This training and reflection session inspired them to stand in others' shoes and think outside the box.

Empathic Modeling

Empathic modeling is a research method and technique for designers to understand users' specific needs, especially for users with disabilities or unique conditions different from designers. The method is easiest to apply when one is designing for people with motor or sensory disabilities, like visual impairment, hearing impairment, and mobility impairment.[18] Students in my course utilized aging simulation costumes, vision impairment goggles and arthritis simulation gloves to experience the emotions and physical conditions some older adults experience on a daily basis. Some students realized it was impossible for them to tie shoelaces wearing arthritis simulation gloves. Some struggled to walk upstairs wearing aging simulation costumes. Some had a hard time using computer screens to study while wearing vision impairment goggles. The empathic modeling experience increased students' awareness and heightened their sensibility to various barriers they often do not realize in everyday life. It opened their minds and prepared them to embrace potential barriers and challenges they might face later in the workshops.

Reflection Writing

During the empathic modeling period, every two students formed a pair to interview and record each other's experiences. After the class, they wrote reflective writing to discuss their observation, experience, and insights. As Atousa Hajshirmohammadi stated, reflection is one of the critical steps associated with experiential learning.[19] This reflection writing assignment helped students to form new knowledge obtained from this experience. In the proceeding activities during this course, including workshops and exhibitions, students wrote reflection writings after each event.

Workshop

Joint workshops connecting students and older adults are essential for the course to succeed. Four workshops, including two in-person and two virtual ones, were designed and hosted. The first two were co-create workshops, where students and older participants from the community used storytelling and co-create toolkits to get to know each other. The next two were co-design workshops, where students discussed the creative solutions with the older adults and built prototypes together. Figure 2.6 illustrates the sequencing of the events in these workshops. We will talk about how to facilitate some of the events in this session.

Meal Together

We started the first workshop with older participants at our community partner Seamaac's community center in south Philadelphia. We provided pastries from a local Chinese bakery that older Asian adults often enjoy. Because of the Covid-19 pandemic regulations in the community center, everyone wore a mask. So we provided options for each participant to bring the pastries home after the event. Older participants appreciated the gesture and loved the snacks, which helped them open up for conversation. For the later in-person workshops, we provided individual lunch boxes so participants had the option to bring them home or eat on site. Food has always been an important part to start our conversation in a casual way.

Storytelling

Good stories not only create a sense of connection but also build trust and unite people together, making people more open to participating and learning from each other.[20] One of the student assignments before the workshops was to create open-ended questions to guide storytelling with older participants. The session was mutual, with both sides telling stories about each other to elicit conversation and build a supporting atmosphere to share. During the session, each older adult was paired with two students from different majors and one bilingual interpreter. Very quickly we realized that the interpreter in a team played a very important role in facilitating the conversation, especially because everyone was wearing masks, so it was hard to see the whole facial expression. The storytelling session was structured in this way: one student led the conversation with the older adult, and the other student recorded the conversation by taking notes, audio, or video recording upon the older participant's agreement beforehand. The interpreter would interpret for both sides while helping to provide explanations and cultural guidance to the students so they could ask culturally appropriate questions and understand the message from older participants. The interpreter also gives context to older participants about students' inquiries. So the role of the interpreter is not simply language translation, but more importantly, facilitating conversation across the barriers on both lingual and cultural levels (refer to Figure 2.7).

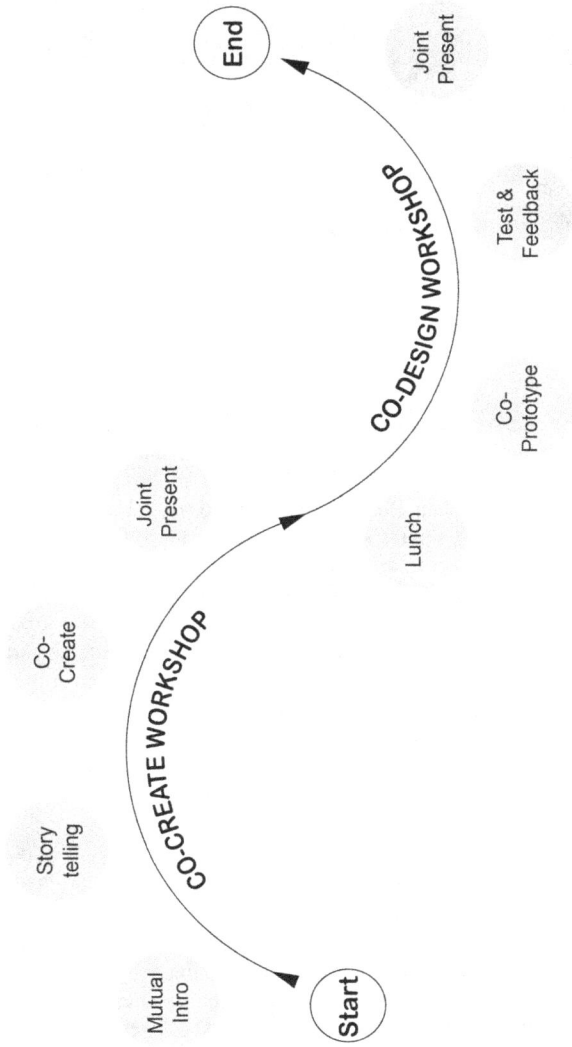

Figure 2.6 Workshop Diagram: sequencing of the events. Created by the author

Figure 2.7 Storytelling session in the workshop. Photo by research assistant Khue Dao

Co-Create Toolkit

Following the course instruction, student teams developed co-create toolkits to bring to the workshop and guided older participants to use them (Figure 2.8). The materials from the co-create toolkits are not general materials. They are culturally relevant elements that help to trigger memories, stories and family relationships. First, students shared with the older adults how they used tools to create their own artwork, like watercolor paint brushes, colored pencils, collaging elements, scissors, glue stickers, fabrics and more. Then, students encouraged older participants to create their own artwork based on what they learned. Together, each intergenerational team created an art piece that conveys a personal story to share with the whole classroom at the end of the workshop. Through this activity, students and older participants learned more about each other and built rapport moving forward to co-design together.

Co-Design Prototyping Kit

Several weeks after the Co-Create workshop, students went back to the community and hosted Co-Design workshops with older participants. This time, students brought prototype materials and encouraged older adults to build the early-stage prototype and discuss their feedback. Prototype kits helped to engage older participants in the process of making and testing, providing guidelines for students to iterate on the concepts. By the end of the workshop, before each team's presentation to the class, one team disappeared. It appeared that the older participant in the team invited the two students and the interpreter to her vegetable garden nearby because this team was working on designing an origami planting pot. The whole team returned with happy smiles.

Figure 2.8 An older adult is using students' co-create toolkits to write calligraphy. Photo by research assistant Khue Dao

Joint Presentation

At the end of each workshop, teams were invited to share their co-created projects and talk about their process. Students and older adults in the teams presented in turn. Each time a student presented in English, the volunteer interpreter in the small team simultaneously interpreted it into the older participant's language, so the older participant could understand. When the older adult presented in their own language, the interpreter presented the same content in English as well. Although it took longer than usual to communicate everyone's ideas to the whole class, students learned that patience in communication is so important to make older adults feel respected and included.

Virtual Platform Zoom

Due to some older adults' concerns about the COVID-19 pandemic, we conducted two virtual workshops with the participants from the Philadelphia Senior Center. To help them obtain the necessary toolkits before the virtual workshop, student teams delivered the toolkits to older adults' homes. Some older adults invited students to tour their home environments, introduced the artworks they were working on, and even packed snacks for students to bring back home. Those casual encounters outside of the classroom brought students and community participants closer, and motivated both sides to contribute to the joint project. Figure 2.9 shows an older participant presenting her collage work through Zoom using materials provided by one student team's co-create toolkit in the virtual workshop. She chose and collaged those images to represent memories of her hometown and youth.

Figure 2.9 Virtual workshop through Zoom

Joint Exhibition

At the end of the semester, a public-facing joint group exhibition opened to the whole Drexel community to showcase the research, products and solutions developed by both students and older adults. The exhibition brought together interdisciplinary students, volunteer interpreters, community members and Drexel faculty, to understand better aging for older Asian immigrant communities. During the exhibition, students hosted workshops with older adults, and both groups exchanged creative works to express appreciation. The final projects include a paper-based planting pot to be constructed with grandchildren, a book with guided prompts offering culturally relevant creative activities, a public park serving the older people living in Chinatown, a website design for older immigrants to find translation services from volunteers, subscription boxes for older adults to use for their hobbies and more. Figure 2.10 captures a corner of the exhibition, with students explaining their projects to the visitors, and older participants viewing and talking about the exhibition together.

Findings

Mood & Mind Mapping

At the beginning of the course, all the students conducted a mood and mind mapping exercise on an online collaborative whiteboard platform. Each student wrote down the first few words or phrases coming to their minds when hearing the word "aging". At the end of the course, students did the same exercise. Comparing the pre-course and post-course results, the conclusion is that students' perceptions towards aging are shifting from mostly negative to mostly positive.

Figure 2.10 Joint Exhibition with students and older adults. Photo by the author

Achievements

Many students and older participants expressed gratitude and appreciated the experiential learning experience from the *Aging & Design* course. Student Isabella Morse, a senior custom design major with concentrations in environmental studies, psychology and design shared her thoughts:

> This class was a unique experience and an amazing learning opportunity. I've learned many little things here and there, from different cultural cues and practices to people's personal traditions. It was all eye-opening. If I had to pick though, the most important thing I've gained is the relationships I was able to make.[21]

One older adult in the course told us:

> Since the Covid-19 pandemic, over two years, the mood of our older community members has been very low. You (students and the instructor) have brought so much joy to our lives and enriched our spirits . . . The events reduced our distance and enhanced the communication between us. I see your efforts in our community, and I cannot express enough gratitude.

Senior product design major student Khue Dao wrote in her reflective writing:

> After each co-design session, my heart is full listening to the older adults. I was able to empathize with their feelings and the hardships that they are facing. One comment really stood out to me was when Mrs. XX said that it was the happiest day that she has ever been able to talk to us, showing hope

for social connections despite the language barrier. It was a memorable experience that I will remember forever and would love nothing more than staying connected with the participants afterward.

Senior student Amjot Malhi from Health Sciences wrote about her experiences:

> Through this experience, I gained invaluable lessons from older adults as it helped me to understand the struggles of an immigrant as it is very difficult to adjust to a new country and culture. I gained a new perspective on how design can positively impact their daily experiences as every age group is different and has different needs. It also helped me to develop more empathy towards older adults and become more aware of the cultural differences that exist in our society. I have understood that it is important to interact with an open mind and engage in meaningful cross-cultural exchanges as people come from diverse continents with various cultures, languages, and traditions.

Architecture graduate student Michael Zhu said,

> In the past, I could not get along well with my grandparents sometimes because I made the assumption that they would never understand me no matter how I explain one thing. After the four workshops, I just suddenly realized I have never tried communicating with my grandparents like the way I elaborated the goal of our group project clearly and patiently (in the Aging & Design course).

Another graduate student from Urban Strategy Theresa Jordan wrote:

> I thought that it was great learning with and from older Asian adults. Some stigmas surrounding aging was completely proven wrong, and it was refreshing to hear their perspective on life and seeing them participate in the activities that we prepared. I really enjoyed listening to their stories and learning about their culture, their hobbies, and what is important to them in life.

The course reflection writing exercise completed by the students demonstrated that the collaboration process developed in the *Aging & Design* course contributed to the students' experiential learning process in significant ways. This cross-cultural co-design collaboration process achieved the following:

- Transcended language, cultural, and generational barriers between the students and older participants
- Amplified marginalized voices from older Asian immigrant communities

- Students gained a foundational understanding of empathic design and the aging process.
- Students increased cultural awareness, evaluated implicit bias and ageism towards an increasingly diverse, older population.
- Interdisciplinary students co-designed with older adults in the community, resulting in innovative age-friendly design solutions.
- Older adults learned creative skills and gained the motivation to explore their passions more.
- Older adults developed unique relationships with the students.
- Laid groundwork for future collaboration between the academic institution and community non-profit organizations

These pedagogical innovations enabled students to empathize with the older community participants and co-design innovative solutions to benefit the community. Most importantly, students achieved transformative learning outcomes at the end of the class, assessed by their reflective writings, course evaluations, and team design project outcomes. The pedagogical innovation motivated participants, young or old, to think beyond their comfort zones. It is now a course that continuously engages students who aim to develop greater empathy and creative skills in their learning process.

Improvements

Since *Aging & Design* is an innovative new course running for the first time, there were many areas the instructor could iterate and improve moving forward. We will focus on a few important ones here.

First, power dynamics between the students and older adult participants in small teams should be addressed moving forward. At the beginning of the course, the instructor formed small teams with two interdisciplinary students, one volunteer interpreter, and one older adult in each team. Students prepared a variety of prompts to engage their older participants, including participatory toolkits and open-ended interview questions. We realized that because of the heavy preparation on the students' side, some teams tend to be one-way communication with mostly students asking older participants questions or guiding them to do things. However, older adults also wanted to ask students questions and get to know them better. Moving forward, we will spend more time giving older adults the opportunity to create their preferred content of communication.

Second, because of the quarter-based structure (10-week course) in the instructor's institution, many students did not have enough time to fully develop their concepts and prototypes. To solve this problem, the instructor is planning to have a sequential course following this one with the entrepreneurial component so students can potentially continue working on their projects, commercialize their solutions and give back to the community. If this were to be replicated in a semester-based structure (approximately 15 weeks), then this problem may not exist.

Third, the most difficult part of the course design is finding enough volunteer interpreters to improve the communication between students and older immigrant participants. Though eventually, each workshop session obtained enough interpreters, it took a great amount of energy and networking to make that happen. For future events, the instructor will consider collaborating with students from the language programs on campus and exploring interpretation devices on the market.

Fourth, a course like this requires a tremendous amount of preparation and facilitation from the instructor, who can easily be burned out from it. It would be more sustainable to delegate tasks to research assistants and teaching assistants to tackle various logistic issues when the framework of the course is defined and tested.

Finally, a new iteration of the course *Creating Age-Friendly Innovations* was launched in the Fall term of 2022, followed by another iteration of *Aging, Design & Entrepreneurship* in the Fall term of 2023. More frameworks and experiences from these courses will be shared in future publications.

Notes

1 Bekki Brau, "Constructivism," in *The Students' Guide to Learning Design and Research*, ed. R. Kimmons (EdTech Books, 2018), accessed January 14, 2023, https://edtechbooks.org/studentguide/constructivism.
2 Saul Mcleod, "Vygotsky's Sociocultural Theory of Cognitive Development," *Simply Psychology*, 2022, accessed January 14, 2023, https://www.simplypsychology.org/vygotsky.html.
3 "Social Constructivism," GSI Teaching Resource Center. University of California, Berkeley, accessed April 29, 2023, https://gsi.berkeley.edu/gsi-guide-contents/learning-theory-research/social-constructivism/.
4 "What Is the Transformative Learning Theory," Western Governors University, 2020, accessed January 14, 2023, https://www.wgu.edu/blog/what-transformative-learning-theory2007.html.
5 Rikke Friis Dam and Teo Yu Siang, "What Is Empathy and Why Is It So Important in Design Thinking?" *The Interaction Design Foundation*, June 10, 2023, https://www.interaction-design.org/literature/article/design-thinking-getting-started-with-empathy.
6 Deana McDonagh et al., "Empathic Design Research: Disability+ Relevant Design," in the *Proceedings of the 8th European Academy of Design Conference: Design Connexity*, Aberdeen Scotland, 1–3, April 1, 2009.
7 "Equity-Centered Design Methodologies," *Bill & Melinda Gates Foundation and Intentional Futures,* accessed June 10, 2023, https://www.designthinkersacademy.co.uk/wp-content/uploads/2022/11/introduction-to-equity-centered-design.pdf.
8 Tania Anaissie et al., "Equity-Centered Design Framework," *Stanford d.school*, June 7, 2021, https://dschool.stanford.edu/resources/equity-centered-design-framework.

9 "Our Approach: A Method for Co-Creating Equitable Outcomes," *Creative Reaction Lab*, accessed June 10, 2023, https://crxlab.org/our-approach.

10 David Kolb, *Experiential Learning: Experience as the Source of Learning and Development* (Englewood Cliffs, NJ: Prentice Hall, 1984), 25–36.

11 Hualin Fu, "What Is the Material Base of Acupuncture? The Nerves!" *Medical Hypotheses* 54, no. 3 (2000): 358–59.

12 "Acupuncture," *Johns Hopkins Medicine*, accessed January 14, 2023, https://www.hopkinsmedicine.org/health/wellness-and-prevention/acupuncture.

13 Richard Buchanan, "Wicked Problems in Design Thinking," *Design Issues* 8, no. 2 (1992): 5–21, accessed April 29, 2023, https://doi.org/10.2307/1511637.

14 Xiaojing Hou, Ruichang Li, and Zhiping Song, "A Bibliometric Analysis of Wicked Problems: From Single Discipline to Transdisciplinarity," *Fudan Journal of the Humanities and Social Sciences* 15, no. 3 (2021): 299–329, accessed April 29, 2023, https://doi.org/10.1007/s40647-022-00346-w.

15 "Meridian (Chinese Medicine)," *Wikimedia Foundation*, last modified January 12, 2023, https://en.wikipedia.org/wiki/Meridian_(Chinese_medicine).

16 "About Art Therapy," *American Art Therapy Association*, January 18, 2023, https://arttherapy.org/about-art-therapy/.

17 Deana McDonagh and Joyce Thomas, "Rethinking Design Thinking: Empathy Supporting Innovation," *AMJ* 3, no. 8 (2010): 458–64, https://doi.org/10.4066/AMJ.2010.391.

18 David Poulson, Martin Ashby, and Simon Richardson, *Userfit: A Practical Handbook on User-Centred Design for Assistive Technology* (Brussels: ECSC-EC-EAEC, 1996), 91–96.

19 Atousa Hajshirmohammadi, "Incorporating Experiential Learning in Engineering Courses," *IEEE Communications Magazine* 55 (2017): 166–69, https://doi.org/10.1109/MCOM.2017.1700373.

20 Vanessa Boris, "What Makes Storytelling So Effective for Learning?" Harvard Business Publishing (Vanessa Boris /wp-content/uploads/2018/12/HBPub-CorpLearn_wide_crimson.svg, 2017), accessed January 14, 2023, https://www.harvardbusiness.org/what-makes-storytelling-so-effective-for-learning/.

21 Laurel Hostak Jones, "Drexel Students Explore Co-Design and Aging in Philadelphia Communities," Westphal College of Media Arts & Design, Drexel University, June 16, 2022, accessed January 14, 2023, https://drexel.edu/westphal/news-events/news/2022/June/Drexel-Students-Explore-Co-Design-and-Aging-in-Philadelphia-Communities/.

Bibliography

American Art Therapy Association. "About Art Therapy." January 18, 2023. https://arttherapy.org/about-art-therapy/.

Anaissie, Tania, Victor Cary, David Clifford, Tom Malarkey, and Susie Wise. "Equity-Centered Design Framework." *Stanford d.school*, June 7, 2021. https://dschool.stanford.edu/resources/equity-centered-design-framework.

Bill & Melinda Gates Foundation and Intentional Futures. "Equity-Centered Design Methodologies." Accessed June 10, 2023. https://www.design

thinkersacademy.co.uk/wp-content/uploads/2022/11/introduction-to-equity-centered-design.pdf.

Boris, Vanessa. "What Makes Storytelling So Effective for Learning?" Harvard Business Publishing. Vanessa Boris /wp-content/uploads/2018/12/HBPub-CorpLearn_wide_crimson.svg,2017.AccessedJanuary14,2023.https://www.harvardbusiness.org/what-makes-storytelling-so-effective-for-learning/.

Brau, B. "Constructivism." In *The Students' Guide to Learning Design and Research*, edited by R. Kimmons. EdTech Books, 2018. Accessed January 14, 2023. https://edtechbooks.org/studentguide/constructivism

Buchanan, Richard. "Wicked Problems in Design Thinking." *Design Issues* 8, no. 2 (1992): 5–21. Accessed April 29, 2023. https://doi.org/10.2307/1511637.

Creative Reaction Lab. "Our Approach: A Method for Co-Creating Equitable Outcomes." Accessed June 10, 2023. https://crxlab.org/our-approach.

Dam, Rikke Friis, and Siang, Teo Yu. "What Is Empathy and Why Is It So Important in Design Thinking?" *The Interaction Design Foundation*, June 10, 2023. https://www.interaction-design.org/literature/article/design-thinking-getting-started-with-empathy.

Fu, Hualin. "What Is the Material Base of Acupuncture? The Nerves!" *Medical Hypotheses* 54, no. 3 (2000): 358–59.

Hajshirmohammadi, Atousa. "Incorporating Experiential Learning in Engineering Courses." *IEEE Communications Magazine* 55 (2017): 166–69. https://doi.org/10.1109/MCOM.2017.1700373.

Hou, Xiaojing, Li, Ruichang, and Song, Zhiping. "A Bibliometric Analysis of Wicked Problems: From Single Discipline to Transdisciplinarity." *Fudan Journal of the Humanities and Social Sciences* 15, no. 3 (2021): 299–329. Accessed April 29, 2023. https://doi.org/10.1007/s40647-022-00346-w.

Johns Hopkins Medicine. "Acupuncture." Accessed January 14, 2023. https://www.hopkinsmedicine.org/health/wellness-and-prevention/acupuncture.

Jones, Laurel Hostak. "Drexel Students Explore Co-Design and Aging in Philadelphia Communities." Westphal College of Media Arts & Design. Drexel University, 2022. Accessed January 14, 2023. https://drexel.edu/westphal/news-events/news/2022/June/Drexel-Students-Explore-Co-Design-and-Aging-in-Philadelphia-Communities/.

Kolb, David. *Experiential Learning: Experience as the Source of Learning and Development*. Englewood Cliffs, NJ: Prentice Hall, 1984.

McDonagh, Deana, Thomas, Joyce. "Rethinking Design Thinking: Empathy Supporting Innovation." *AMJ* 3, no. 8 (2010): 458–64. https://doi.org/10.4066/AMJ.2010.391

McDonagh, Deana, Thomas, Joyce, Chen, Siying, He, June, Hong, Yong Seok, Kim, Yunjin, Zhang, Zhongren, and Feniosky, Pena-Mora. "Empathic Design Research: Disability+ Relevant Design." In the *Proceedings of the 8th European Academy of Design Conference: Design Connexity*, Aberdeen Scotland, 1–3, April 1, 2009.

Mcleod, Saul. "Vygotsky's Sociocultural Theory of Cognitive Development." *Simply Psychology*, 2022. Accessed January 14, 2023. https://www.simplypsychology.org/vygotsky.html.

Poulson, D., M. Ashby, and S. Richardson, eds. *USERfit. A Practical Handbook on User-Centred Design for Assistive Technology.* Brussels-Luxembourg: TIDEEC-DG XIII, ECSC-EC-EAEC, 1996.

"Social Constructivism." GSI Teaching Resource Center. University of California, Berkeley. Accessed April 29, 2023. https://gsi.berkeley.edu/gsi-guide-contents/learning-theory-research/social-constructivism/.

"What Is the Transformative Learning Theory." Western Governors University, 2020. Accessed January 14, 2023. https://www.wgu.edu/blog/what-transformative-learning-theory2007.html.

Wikimedia Foundation. "Meridian (Chinese Medicine)." Last modified January 12, 2023. https://en.wikipedia.org/wiki/Meridian_(Chinese_medicine).

3 Creative and Intellectual Resilience

A New Agenda for Architectural Education

Siobhan Barry

The Biosocial Model

Architecture is a complex course, rarely studied formally at school. Generally speaking, the cohort intake has been used to achieving excellent results throughout their education,[1] yet the course while academically taxing, is often considered both subjective and creative. There have been many studies undertaken regarding the mental health impacts on student well-being while at university;[2] however, architecture students invariably undertake a course of greater length and intensity, and then upon graduation face increased job insecurity,[3] more so than comparable graduate professions. This means graduates will need to prepare and maintain a skill set in constant flux, the implied insecurity of this situation is not without associated psychological and practical risks and consequences. Perceived well-being among the student population is a cause for concern, as architectural educators, clearly this situation requires a pedagogical response. CASEL a collaborative for academic, social and emotional learning at the University of Illinois have noted that "resilience education is a component of positive education".[4] As such it is the contention of the author that the theory, practice and pursuit of resilience training embedded into architecture studio projects and culture promises to positively enhance the academic potential of a very capable and creative cohort.

The Biosocial Education Model posited by Youdell engages with the sociology of education's contemporary interests using assemblage and complexity theory as a basis for evaluating educational and pedagogic phenomena.[5] Often used in a therapeutic setting for personal growth and well-being, the biopsychosocial model has a much-needed place in an educational setting. Biosocial research unsettles the neat distinction between a person who is social and a body which is biological. Informed by understandings of complexity, forming the development of concepts and methods that reach across domains to explore the interactions of diverse influences and processes.

Architectural education is itself a complex biosocial phenomenon; approaching architectural pedagogy in this way has the capacity to positively limit inequalities by enhancing the learning process. In relation to the

DOI: 10.4324/9781032705927-4

project, evaluating student reaction and response using the biosocial model was critical in the groupwork pedagogy toolkit, encouraging stages of growth and development, particularly in dealing with unmoderated public responses outside of the studio. However, effective pedagogical constructs should challenge and affect change in relation to learning opportunities. Personality type learning styles are not static "perhaps the most popular [neuro]myth is that a student learns most effectively when they are taught in their preferred learning style",[6] instead processes are mobile and can change in context and in relation to learning opportunities.

As Hynes et al. have noted, learning is itself a form of adaptive behavior that is both "exogenously and endogenously produced by intervention and by design"[7] as such pedagogically, live projects offer an opportunity to engage in this behavior in a more stimulating and dynamic environment, outside of and adjacent to the formal studio setting. Live projects are inherently contextual, totally dependent on the conditions and time context in which they are conceived and operate – The Pavilion Project, a collaboration with the National Trust was no exception.

Cross Collaboration: The Live Project

The live project is nothing new in schools of architecture.[8] They are at once a valuable tool in the arsenal of architectural education and a complex and confounding system of multiple moving parts, placing the student at the center of this mode of teaching, facilitating and celebrating collaboration. The experience of translating a design from a piece of paper to a full scale realized work, interpolating building construction from a technology lecture to a final form capable of withstanding environmental and physical stresses and strains for a public site is clearly a challenge. Yet the experiences of teamwork and physical labor and of quickly resolving complex, multivariable problems in a spatial context so that work can proceed, as Wilder has observed, "reinforce different ways of understanding architecture".[9] Relying on an iterative design process, the live project as pedagogy is essentially about developing, using and maintaining an effective design methodology, blurring the distinction between process and product, creating a natural setting for a "situated, critical and inclusive education".[10]

Project Outline

The second-year undergraduate study of architecture in the UK is a critical period of personal, professional and social development. Students often approach it with mixed feelings of confidence, optimism and sometimes nascent stirrings of imposter syndrome. The glue that connects the foundations of earlier study to the final flourish of their graduating year. Considerable nervous energy needs to be well directed and handled with care. The key to success at this stage is adaptability and engagement beyond the comfort zone. One way to achieve this is to introduce an element of risk and exposure to unpredictable critique; the live project.

The Pavilion Project at Manchester School of Architecture (MSA), in partnership with the National Trust, was designed as a situated learning environment employing "legitimate peripheral participation"[11] as espoused by Lave and Wenger. Second-year undergraduate architecture students from Manchester School of Architecture were tasked with designing and building pavilions for the Winter Gardens at Dunham Massey, Cheshire, UK capable of architecturally interpreting the historic site and creating a dialogue with visitors to the property. This was the first project the students had undertaken taking up the first six weeks of the autumn term. Founded in 1895, The National Trust is an independent charity for environmental and heritage conservation in England, Wales and Northern Ireland. The Trust owns over 500 heritage properties and is responsible for their maintenance and upkeep, many of which include historic houses and gardens, industrial monuments and social history sites.[12] As such, working with the most high-profile heritage conservation charity in the UK provided students from the school of architecture with a unique opportunity to work collaboratively on a live project with a respected and high-profile client. The brief required a pavilion design that would enhance the natural beauty of the historic site and engage the 350,000 annual visitors to the property. It must respect the natural environment of the site and Dunham Massey's architectural heritage, meeting the demanding levels of rigor, taste and technical skill demonstrated by the National Trust team at Dunham Massey.

The rapid turnaround of the project from launch to installation on site meant that dynamics of group work were continually tested and re-evaluated to contextualize perceptions of success and ownership of the concept, bridging the real and the hypothetical.[13] The project explored not only conservation in terms of respect to site, but also required a synergistic confluence of skills, through the design, manufacture and construction process. Added to this were the vagaries of a live build, with a very short window from initial design to completion on site. As Morrow has observed, providing demanding time constraints applied to a live project "can intensify [the student's] connections to their own learning and to the role of architecture".[14] The tight time frame, although challenging, allowed for students to communicate authentic, unrestricted responses to the client's needs and the brief. Whereas a longer project may have encouraged students to "acquire the clients' brief and retreat into the academy",[15] there was not enough time here for students to illegitimately possess the project, allowing the client to remain in the driving seat.

The brief looked at the way a live build would be received, critiqued and questioned in a public capacity outside of an exclusively educational forum, and ultimately changed the way in which students interpreted critique and success, establishing resilience and group accountability in the cohort. The design and construction elements of the project were consciously designed to provide the students involved with professional and psychological agency; drawing out experiences, knowledge and skills that are not exposed, utilized or valorized in normative design studio models.[16] This quickly became one of the most extraordinary pedagogical construction projects the school had ever undertaken.

The project took six weeks from brief delivery to on-site construction, a personally relevant and highly motivated challenge, and was made up of four phases. In phase one, after a site visit to the National Trust property, each student in a cohort of approximately 200 designed a pavilion for a designated site determined by the head gardener and her team in the Winter Gardens at Dunham Massey. The brief stated that the pavilion design should in some way refer to the gardens, the site, Dunham Massey Hall's historical and conservational significance, a part of its collection or the family who once owned the site. The designs were then presented to their studio groups of approximately 22 students and 2 staff who evaluated the projects, bringing two forward from each studio group for a whole year exhibition (week one) (Figure 3.1). At this point students had to challenge their own thinking and develop a new strategy. Previously they were considering their own design unilaterally and proposing their concept in a small studio group setting. The students had to decide as a group of former individual ideas which proposition, or hybrid thereof, stood the best chance to bring forward to the next stage for the benefit of the whole group (Figure 3.1). There was the potential here for egos, hurt feelings or social pressure to come into play, which was tempered by the roles played by staff as expert advisors. Rather than simply judging and choosing, staff facilitated an inclusive discussion and strategic deliberation process, creating an expansive space for the acceptance and deliberation of competing ideas. This approach facilitated students to move out of their comfort zone to endure a controlled discomfort. Critically it is at these liminal edge conditions of comfort where intellectual, creative and emotional growth takes place, establishing resilience. As Irvine suggests "by undertaking acts of voluntary discomfort we harden ourselves against misfortunes that might befall us in the future".[17] This stage of the project began to reveal the diversity of skills and experience within the group, some of which would otherwise remain latent in a desk study. It was important for students to experience and realize that is how groups thrive or struggle, while simultaneously developing their own voice. This observation of variety and exchange would become one of the strengths of the project.

Architectural competitions are commonplace in the profession. By adding a competitive element into the brief structure, students were afforded an opportunity to engage competitively, both individually and collectively, addressing the human inclination for social learning.[18] As the project progressed, students began to realize that the sense of competition lessened, and a sense of collective endeavor took over. Constructing the learning experience

to address the three psychological needs of self-determination theory (autonomy, competence and relatedness), increased student satisfaction, their sense
of individual and collective well-being and positively impacted motivational
drivers for the project. The tempering of competitiveness so that the project
delivery remained motivational rather than problematic, was keenly moni-
tored by staff and by the students themselves.

Following Biggs' constructive alignment pedagogical approach, where
learning outcomes, teaching and learning activities and assessment are integrated,[19] studio groups were divided into two cohorts concentrating their
efforts on developing the selected designs to produce a 1:50 scale model and at
least three competition style presentation boards for the year-wide exhibition.

Figure 3.1 Whole year project exhibition, Manchester School of Architecture. Pavilion
project peer review process – students were asked to objectively critique the
work of the whole student cohort, completing peer review and voting forms
to select the pavilion design they considered best fit the client requirements
and brief. Photograph by the author

Figure 3.2 Group project presentation to the National Trust team from Dunham Massey, Holden Gallery, Manchester Metropolitan University. Photograph by the author

Phase two culminated in a display and year-wide review, with second-year students reflectively critiquing each other's designs and voting for the most successful project based upon the brief. One design from each studio group was taken forward for presentation to the National Trust team at Dunham Massey, comprised of the deputy head gardener and visitor experience officers (weeks two and three) (Figure 3.2). After detailed review and feedback from the National Trust team as well as MSA staff, six pavilion designs were chosen to be taken forward to Phase 3 – material sourcing, resource funding, construction design and development and prototype testing (weeks 4 and 5). The theme of problem-solving was central to the effective delivery of the project; students were expected to identify problems, especially regarding construction, material or time frame limitations and propose a design solution that would work with the demands of the brief.

Construction Organization

The construction phase of the project was developed in the studio and workshops at Manchester School of Architecture. Each student group was responsible for self-organizing into project teams with specific roles in the design, production, finishing and construction of each pavilion. Models and maquettes were produced to test and refine the structure of the pavilions selected by the National Trust team. Due to size and complexity of building and delivering six large-scale pavilion designs within a strictly limited time frame, the project demanded each pavilion structure be constructed of demountable component parts for ease of storage within studio and workshop spaces and for transportation to the site. Each student team was required to fully assemble their pavilion in the studio space at MSA prior to delivery to check for any structural issues (Figure 3.3). Staff were also able to rehearse and time assembly sequences in response to the client request of a short site assembly window and to mitigate any health, safety or practical issues which might have been unresolved before delivery to site. This process of testing and re-evaluating their designs provided the students with an immediate ground for self-evaluation. The engagement processes necessitated by the fabrication component of the project contributed to a positive learning cycle, where feedback was obtained is situ, in real time where construction issues were identified and addressed, and the designs adapted accordingly. As identified by Lave and Wenger,[20] this iterative process was significant by not only its authentic context, but also by the learner willingly absorbing information that went on to inform future practice and their own critical judgment.

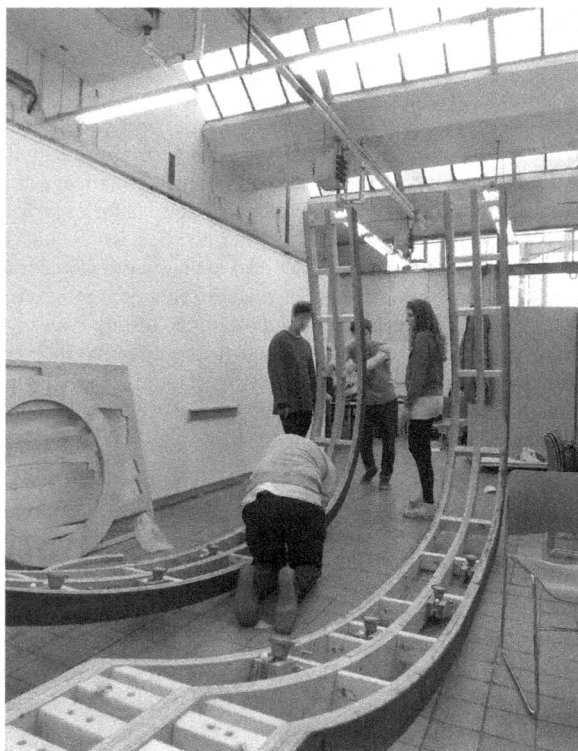

Figure 3.3 Pavilion test construction, Chime Pavilion, Manchester School of Architecture. Photograph by the author

The sites selected by the National Trust within the Winter Garden at Dunham Massey could not be directly accessed by vehicular traffic; therefore, the designs needed to address the challenges of site access and material delivery. Component parts needed to be transported to each site either by hand or by wheelbarrow (Figure 3.4). Despite these demands, the student site teams remained highly motivated and enjoyed the challenge, creating stimulating debate and scenario planning, actively challenging the concept of a problem and reframing it as a design driver.

Critical Reflections

It is fair to say that students involved in the project exhibited what Donald Schön has described as the "wicked problems of the design studio";[21] however, in this case the heroic amount of time, ingenuity, pride and other resources the students poured into this project over a very short period, produced a meaningful contribution to the visitor experience at Dunham Massey. Educationally, the project provided students with a meaningful experience of the tangible dynamism of the built environment and the resilience to author construction solutions to issues that arose. The project promoted wider engagement and feedback from internal and external sources and increased social support between peers. Central to the success of the project was the creation of a supportive environment within the studio. The sense that both

Figure 3.4 Pavilion sectional elements being carried to site. Extremely limited access and ground conditions meant students had to physically maneuver elements into position for final assembly. Winter Gardens, Dunham Massey, Altrincham, Cheshire. Photograph by the author

staff and students were in it together and would do what had to be done in order for the project to succeed, was found to increase the student's belief in their own ability and motivation, which if not present, has been found to inhibit the creative process.[22] Phase four saw the pavilion construction on site (Figures 3.5 and 3.6), where time was very limited due to the National Trust's proviso that all construction work should be completed in time for the gardens to open to members of the public. This added demonstrable real world pressure; however, the tight time frame and professional expectation of working with a live client, proved to be a critical factor in the effectiveness of the learning and teaching approach.[23]

Throughout, students were supported by a dedicated and engaged staff team who continually provided positive encouragement and belief in students' abilities. This in turn led to more productivity, and upon critical reflection, the improved well-being of the students involved.[24] As Zeidner and Endler have noted, how an individual copes with stress determines their well-being,[25] and this was evident when evaluating this project. The live project was purposefully not concluded by a traditional critique, but rather a public celebration of the achievements of the whole group. This transformed what would usually be an in-house, closed critique that exists in the design studio into an open, cultural event for everyone who took part or supported them throughout the project. After on-site completion, the students involved were asked to critically reflect upon and appraise their group work, design, effective working practice and positive versus constructive feedback from staff and visitors to

Figure 3.5 Octavia Pavilion under construction, Dunham Massey, Altrincham, Cheshire. Photograph by the author

Figure 3.6 Strata Pavilion under construction, Winter Garden, Dunham Massey, Altrincham, Cheshire. Photograph by the author

the property. Feelings of stress were discussed largely in a positive manner with an overall sense that while stress was experienced, it was harnessed to positive effect, and they shared pride in the resultant outcome. Throughout the project students exhibited a learned resourcefulness, enabling an effective critical reflection of their contribution to the project. This reflective approach was an important aspect of effective pedagogy.[26] Effective learning requires pedagogies that offered intellectual quality, connectedness to learners' worlds (creating a design that would engage them as well as visitors to the property), a supportive learning environment in studio and on site, and a valuing of and working with difference.[27] Here feeling efficacious became a central asset in prioritizing both life and academic events and was carried through into their final year of undergraduate study.

Live Project Resilience

Resilience is defined by Folke as "the capacity of a system to absorb disturbances and reorganise while undergoing change, so as to retain essentially the same function, structure, identity of feedbacks".[28] Resilience is a core component of psychological well-being and has been found to have positive competencies in the stress coping process. Economically, resilience is defined as the "efficient use of remaining resources at a given point in time to produce as much as possible, expediating resources and rapidly adapting to change";[29] this definition is particularly apt when evaluating the Pavilion Project. The live build project essentially embedded resilience training into the student cohort's project brief and educational experience explicitly due to several factors. Working with a prominent live client with exacting expectations of design, build quality and longevity as well as engaging with many visitors to the site, in addition to the quick project timeline enabled what Luthar and Ciachetti have termed "positive adaptation"[30] exhibited across the student cohort despite the presence of risk (project failure) or adversity (difficulties building on site). Continued critical reflection played a key role in the design of the project, enabling students to understand and reflect upon "processes contributing to positive adjustment under conditions of adversity" broadening their understanding of developmental processes that may not be evident in "good enough" normative environments.[31]

The character, trait or situational premise of resiliency is that people possess selective strengths or assets to help them survive adversity. While architecture as a university course is not seen as a potentially adverse situation, personal strengths and skills frequently mentioned across resilience literature are eminently applicable to architectural education:

- Emotional competence – emotion awareness and regulation
- Self-regulation – impulse control, goal setting, self-discipline, perseverance
- Problem-solving and decision-making – being able to think creatively, flexibly and realistically about any problems encountered
- Social awareness – perspective taking, empathy, respect for others
- Social competence – communication, social engagement, teamwork, conflict management, giving and receiving help
- Self-efficacy, optimism, sense of purpose or meaning
- Personal skills and strengths, for example, self-control, problem-solving and optimism – linked to higher academic achievement and greater emotional well-being[32]

Iterative Process of Creative Resilience

Live studio and interactive build projects often have a complex interwoven relationship and can be somewhat contradictory by nature. They must simultaneously be real enough for the yet un-qualified architectural student, while being generally small scale, self-sufficient in nature, somewhat self-directed in addressing solutions to unexpected problems, but with enough complexity of real-world learning, plus the added complexity and the associated risk of a real client. Employing the biosocial model as an evaluative tool, the live project had a positive impact on interpersonal skills, conflict management and group work, creating a community of practice[33] and positively impacting student satisfaction and sense of well-being. This directly correlates with Engeström's activity theory of learning, where an individual's relationship to their environment is mediated by their community, making a three-way relationship of mutual mediation, as the community's relationship with its environment is mediated by individuals and the individuals' relationship with their community is mediated by the environment.[34] Activity theory provides a conceptual framework to understand the interrelationship between activities, actions, operations and artifacts, subjects' motives and goals and aspects of the social, organizational and societal contexts within which these activities are framed. Using this premise as a reflective tool, it is possible to map the goals, limitations, constraints and rules imposed by the live project upon the undergraduate student collective, with resilience training supplanting Engeström's tool at the peak of the pyramid (Figure 3.7).

Here, activity theory is more than a modeling approach used in hypothetical desk studies. The live project scenario fits into the practice-theoretic base: using the systemic construct of activity to represent, in a compact, structured form, group collective practices. In this sense, project inception, iterative development and a group sense of ownership become motivational objectives performed by subjects in a mediated context, "the on site build". A live project has many moving parts, the complexity of which ebbs and flows throughout, central to the successful completion which is the creation of a system capable of self-organizing. Change and innovation are not the results of a specific individuals' action or vision, but of developed contradictions to which individuals and the collective group respond, a feedback response developed through a pattern of resilient behaviors. An *expansive transformation* of the activity occurs when, after contradictions emerge, the object of the activity (live project) is reconceptualized to embrace a radically broader horizon of problems and possibilities.[35] The physical sciences provide evidence for the necessity of a by-design conferral of resilience to sustain a system. Systemic capacity for resilience is a recurring theme in complex systems: system collapse is likely to occur over a given period of time without the structural and material capacity for recovery and adaptation to disruption.[36] Ungar has identified seven common principles of resilience, all applicable in a live project scenario:

1. Resilience occurs in contexts of adversity (challenge).
2. Resilience is a process.
3. There are trade-offs between systems when a system experiences resilience.

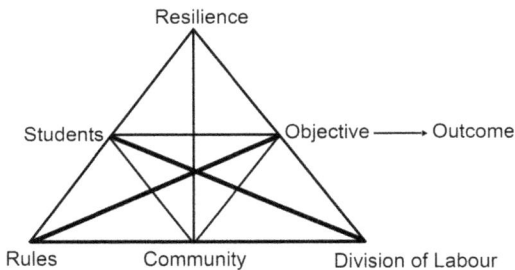

Figure 3.7 Resilience/Activity diagram after Engeström

4. A resilient system is open, dynamic and complex.
5. A resilient system promotes connectivity.
6. A resilient system demonstrates experimentation and learning.
7. A resilient system includes diversity, redundancy and participation.[37]

Self-Regulation

Beyond a hypothetical project brief, the real world is fundamentally dynamic, with systems constantly changing and adapting to shifting incentives and constraints. The definition of economic resiliency refers to a system functioning and adapting to shock; in essence the Pavilion Project could be defined as a series of micro shocks to the student psyche, who in turn had to rapidly adapt to unforeseen obstacles growing in resiliency throughout. The process-based nature of this project saw a model of resiliency applied to both the design process through continual iterative development, culminating in a live build, and to the process of self-reflection and development.

Resilience skills do not necessarily automatically transfer from one situation to another, which is why a range of situations and scenarios were designed so that students could develop agency in different capacities, enabling more people to find a valued position in the broad church of architectural education.[38] A change or a turning point in teaching methodology can help to crystallize thinking and perspectives that may not have been considered before. Continually revisiting and evaluating their performance throughout the project afforded students to determine patterns of skill, effectiveness or opportunity, this in turn leading to the ability to forward plan or envisage adversity, further developing resilience strengths. The continued analysis of this project applied a method of systemic resilience; this consisted of two distinct and interrelated approaches: Systemic Resilience by Design (RBD) and Systemic Resilience by Intervention (RBI). Students were briefed at the beginning of the project that their objective was twofold: to design and build with a live client, but also (and arguably more importantly) to develop a practice of creative and professional resiliency. They were reminded that while acting with their own personal agency, they were part of a group, or ecosystem if you will, that exists with its complexity and interconnectedness. Personal risks become absorbed into the team system, helping students to focus on whether their present skills were sufficient to deal with the current scenario.

At a very early stage in the project, it was determined that it was necessary that a considerable number of proposals would not proceed to the next stage. This resilience by design (RBD) strategy allowed students the opportunity to reflect upon their performance and swiftly address their individual disappointment while focusing on their groups overall progress to the next stage of competition, in which they would play a different, but equally valid role. This approach reduced the capacity for the student to over think or ruminate on their perceived failure, but instead allowed them to exert control over events, finding a path out of their present predicament and maintaining control. This monitoring of response to micro adversity allowed for incremental resilient growth.[39]

Liminal Growth Attitude

Attitude is the heart of resilience. Throughout the project student groups were challenged by shifting parameters in their design exploration, continually pushing them to the limits of what was understood as comfortable. Liminality is understood as a period of transition between socially defined conditions characterized by imbalance. Liminal growth, therefore, is a phenomenon by which resilience is developed at the ambiguous edges of the comfort zone, facilitating students to think critically and develop discernment in both their product and practice. Towards the later stages of the project, it became clear to students that working for shared goals meant being part of something beyond themselves, establishing a critically important sense of belonging, duality of identity and common responsibility and success. Having established support from others and a degree of self-acceptance, the ongoing project afforded students the capacity to develop higher frustration tolerance, perspective maintenance and emotional regulation. When circumstances became challenging, these were met with good humor on the part of staff by whom it was important to model similar levels of frustration tolerance and adaptability to maintain a sense of curiosity and perseverance in the student cohort. All the behaviors described above being key indicators of both resilience and positive psychology.

Building on site was for many students their first experience of actual construction and its associated stressors. Physically constructing their designs in a real-world scenario allowed them to find meaning in their design in addition to addressing and resolving any pitfalls. It was at this stage particularly that there was a shifting balance of strengths, both throughout the cohort and on an individual or personal level for each student, establishing resilience by intervention (RBI). Using tools in the rain and giving and taking instruction from teammates under time pressure and with public scrutiny, was inevitably more challenging for some more than others, but for everyone involved, it was a turning point in which the three Is as described by Grotberg were considered. Students were asked to consider to what extent

I have (external support)
I am (inner strengths)
I will (social and problem-solving skills)[40]

These three assertions formed the basis of an informal assessment at this point.

It was at this stage that the cohort dynamic shifted once again in interrelatedness and complexity, as students with particular skill sets were identified and sought out by other groups building in different locations on the National Trust site. Skills and roles were exchanged as the larger group coalesced to increase more effective productivity of the discreet builds, building cohort level resilience displaying characteristics of trust, autonomy identity and initiative industry.[41] Issues of teamwork, identity and effectiveness were all experienced positively and negatively, and they were tasked to monitor and reflect on this dynamic with as much diligence as the architectural intervention. The pavilion design may be site specific, but the transferrable skill set, experience and networks made during the project are still referenced positively long after its conclusion.

Conclusion

It is the meanings (attitudes and beliefs) that we attach to events and not the event themselves that largely determine how we react to them. When students' design endeavors remain comfortably hypothetical, so can the meanings they attach to the exercise. Putting students into a real-world project scenario, the attitudes, beliefs and consequently meanings they attach to it are more impactful. Of the many diverse interpretations of resilience methodologies, they all agree that resilience is not a fixed personality trait, but instead the result of a process – a skill set born of practice. That process is not developed in social isolation; just like in the architecture studio it is relational and experiential. Psychologically, emotional response is linked to significance and tied to learning, thus in a live project situation, emotional responses and consequently learning potential are heightened as the significance of events is no longer hypothetical, correlating to Engeström's theory of expansion as a "thoughtfully mastered learning activity".[42] It is argued throughout this chapter that resilience is ordinary, not extraordinary. The common adage that no experience is wasted if you learn from it is exceptionally true here, but often the memory or meaning is something retrieved in the long term and not immediately clear at the time, much like the iterative process of design. When extraordinary experiences are made more meaningful by virtue of their reality, learning can occur on several levels and is reflected upon with more immediate clarity by virtue of its intensity – resilience by design.

Architectural education pedagogies have had to rapidly adapt due to the Covid 19 pandemic. Repeated lockdowns meant that undertaking something as physically engaging as a live project was impossible. Limitations on social distancing meant that the real interpersonal skill set and expectations changed. Continued evolution meant formally acknowledging and making space for resilience of both staff and students in architectural education. The global pandemic has proven that the cannon of knowledge, theory, and critical thinking can, and must, embrace this concept in order to fully serve and sustain the contemporary and future architectural educational experience and practice. Moving forward, creative resilient educative pedagogies devised through the pandemic should be harnessed and applied to team building and personal development skills. Whether working as a group in a team or individually, personal accountability and adaptability (resilience) are central to both realities. Contemporary pedagogical practice is likely to require, and must provide, a mixture of hybrid working going forward. Through an evaluation of the Pavilion Project, some value was derived from embedded resilience training in all but name. Post pandemic, it is time to add these skills consciously and explicitly into the undergraduate architecture curriculum, creating the foundation for a new conceptual framework bearing in mind the philosophy, ethics and consideration of such an ethos as part of a proactively received and engaged student experience.

Notes

1 Rashida Ng, "What Will It Take? Reflections on Diversity, Equality and Inclusion in Architectural Education," *Journal of Architectural Education* 73, no. 2 (2019): 142.
2 See Serap Akgun and Joseph Ciarrochi, "Learned Resourcefulness Moderates the Relationship Between Academic Stress and Academic Performance," *Educational Psychology* 23, no. 3 (2003) and Gary Felsten and Kathy Wilcox, "Influences of Stress and Situation-Specific Mastery Beliefs and Satisfaction with Social Support on Well-being and Academic Performance," *Psychological* Reports 70 (1992).
3 Leonard Bachman and Christine Bachman, "Student Perceptions of Academic Workload in Architectural Education," *Journal of Architectural and Planning Research* 23, no. 4 (2006): 278.
4 CASEL Briefs, *Background on Social and Emotional Learning (SEL)* (Chicago: University of Illinois, 2007), 2.
5 Deborah Youdell, "Bioscience and the Sociology of Education: The Case for Biosocial Education," *British Journal of Sociology of Education* 38, no. 8 (2017): 1273.
6 Paul Howard-Jones, "Neuroscience and Education: Myths and Messages," *Nature Reviews Neuroscience* 15 (2014): 817.
7 William Hynes, Benjamin D. Trump, Alan Kirman, Andrew Haldane, and Igor Linkov, "Systemic Resilience in Economics," *Nature Physics* 18 (2022): 381–84.
8 See Johann Albrecht, "Towards a Theory of Participation in Architecture – An Examination of Humanistic Planning Theories," *Journal of Architectural Education* 42, no. 1 (1988): 24–31; Jori Erdman and Robert Weddle, "Designing/Building/Learning," *Journal of Architectural Education* 55, no. 3 (2002): 174–79; Kathleen Watt and Derek Cottrell, "Grounding the Curriculum: Learning from Live Projects in Architectural Education," *International Journal of Learning* 13 (2006): 97–104; Ruth Morrow, "Creative Transformations," in *Design Studio Pedagogy: Horizons for the Future*, ed. Ashraf Salama and Nicholas Wilkinson (Gateshead: The Urban International Press, 2007), 100–14; Ruth Morrow and James Benedict Brown, "Live Projects as Critical Pedagogies," in *Live Projects: Designing with People*, ed. Melanie Dodd, Fiona Harrisson, and Esther Charlesworth (Melbourne: RMIT Press, 2012), 232–47.

9 Lynnette Wilder, "What Belongs to Architecture: Teaching Construction among Live Projects," in *Architecture Live Projects: Pedagogy into Practice*, ed. Harriet Harriss and Lynette Wilder (New York: Routledge, 2014), 33.

10 Morrow and Brown, "Live Projects as Critical Pedagogies," 236.

11 Jean Lave and Etienne Wenger, *Situated Learning: Legitimate Peripheral Participation* (Cambridge: Cambridge University Press, 1991), 95.

12 National Trust, *National Trust Annual Report 20–21 [PDF]* (Swindon, UK: National Trust Publications, 2021), accessed January 4, 2023.

13 Ashraf Salama and Michael J. Crosbie, eds., "Design Education: Explorations and Prospects for a Better Built Environment," *ArchNet I-JAR: International Journal of Architectural Research* 4, no. 2–3 (2010): 14.

14 Ruth Morrow, "Architecture from the Dogs . . .," in *Radical Pedagogies: Architectural Education and the British Tradition*, ed. Daisy Froud and Harriet Harriss (London: RIBA Publishing, 2015), 115–21.

15 Ibid.

16 Morrow and Brown, "Live Projects as Critical Pedagogies," 242.

17 William Irvine, *A Guide to the Good Life: The Ancient Art of Stoic Joy* (Oxford: Oxford University Press, 2009), 112.

18 Gergely Csibra and Gyorgy Gergely, "Social Learning and Social Cognition: The Case for Pedagogy," in *Processes of Change in Brain and Cognitive Development. Attention and Performance, XXI*, ed. Yuko Munakata and Mark Johnson (Oxford: Oxford University Press, 2006), 249.

19 John Biggs, "Constructive Alignment in University Teaching," *HERDSA Review of Higher Education* 1 (1999).

20 Lave and Wenger, *Situated Learning*, 81.

21 Donald Schön, *The Design Studio: An Exploration of its Traditions and Potentials* (London: RIBA Publications, 1985).

22 Carl Bereiter and Marlene Scardamalia, "Intentional Learning as a Goal of Instruction," in *Knowing, Learning and Instruction: Essays in Honour of Robert Glaser*, ed. Lauren Resnick (Hillside, NJ: Lawrence Erlbaum Associates, 1989), 361.

23 Akgun and Ciarrochi, "Learned Resourcefulness Moderates the Relationship between Academic Stress and Academic Performance," 122.

24 Carl A. Smith and Mark E. Boyer, "Adapted Verbal Feedback, Instructor Interaction of Student Emotions in the Landscape Architecture Studio," *International Journal of Art and Design Education* 34, no. 2 (2015): 270.

25 Moshe Zedner and Norman Endler, eds., *Handbook of Coping: Theory, Research, Applications* (New York: John Wiley and Sons, 1996), 9.

26 Mary James and Andrew Pollard, "TRLP's Ten Principles for Effective Pedagogy: Rationale, Development, Evidence, Argument and Impact," *Research Papers in Education* 26, no. 3 (2011): 286.

27 Bob Lingard, Martin Mills, and Debra Hayes, "Teachers and Productive Pedagogies: Contextualising, Conceptualising, Utilising," *Pedagogy Culture and Society* 11, no. 3 (2003).

28 Carl Folke, "Resilience (Republished)," *Ecology and Society* 21, no. 4 (2016): 44.

29 Hynes et al., "Systemic Resilience in Economics," 381.

30 Suniya Luthar, Dante Cicchetti, and Bronwyn Becker, "The Construct of Resilience: A Critical Evaluation and Guidelines for Future Work," *Child Development* 71, no. 3 (2000): 543–62.
31 Ibid., 552.
32 Glenn E. Richardson, "The Metatheory of Resilience and Resiliency," *Journal of Clinical Psychology* 58, no. 3 (2002): 243.
33 Deborah Youdell and Martin R. Lindley, *Biosocial Education: The Social and Biological Entanglements of Learning* (New York: Routledge, 2018), 129.
34 Yrjö Engeström, "Activity Theory and Individual and Social Transformation," in *Perspectives on Activity Theory*, ed. Yrjö Engeström, Reijo Miettinen, and Raija-Leena Punamaki (Cambridge: Cambridge University Press, 1999).
35 Emmanuel D. Adamides, "Activity Theory for Understanding and Managing System Innovations," *International Journal of Innovation Studies* 7, no. 2 (2023): 129.
36 Hynes et al., "Systemic Resilience in Economics," 381–84.
37 Michael Ungar, "Systemic Resilience: Principles and Processes for a Science of Change in Contexts of Adversity," *Ecology and Society* 23, no. 4 (2018), https://www.jstor.org/stable/26796886.
38 Morrow, "Architecture from the Dogs . . .," 118.
39 Edith Grotberg, ed., *Resilience for Today: Gaining Strength from Adversity* (Westport: Praeger, 2003), 20.
40 Edith Grotberg, "Countering Depression with the Five Building Blocks of Resilience," *Reaching Today's Youth* 4, no. 1 (1999): 67.
41 Ibid.
42 Yrjö Engeström, *Learning by Expanding: An Activity Theoretical Approach to Developmental Research* (Helsinki: Orienta-Konsultit, 1987), 210.

Bibliography

Adamides, Emmanuel D. "Activity Theory for Understanding and Managing System Innovations." *International Journal of Innovation Studies* 7, no. 2 (2023).
Akgun, Serap, and Joseph Ciarrochi. "Learned Resourcefulness Moderates the Relationship between Academic Stress and Academic Performance." *Educational Psychology* 23, no. 3 (2003).
Albrecht, Johann. "Towards a Theory of Participation in Architecture – An Examination of Humanistic Planning Theories." *Journal of Architectural Education* 42, no. 1 (1988): 24–31.
Bachman, Leonard, and Christine Bachman. "Student Perceptions of Academic Workload in Architectural Education." *Journal of Architectural and Planning Research* 23, no. 4 (2006).
Biggs, John. "Constructive Alignment in University Teaching." *HERDSA Review of Higher Education* 1 (1999).
Boyer, Ernest L., and Lee D. Mitgang. *Building Community: A New Future for Architecture Education and Practice: A Special Report.* Princeton, NJ: Carnegie Foundation for the Advancement of Teaching, 1996.

Casakin, Hernan P. "Metaphors in Design Problem-solving: Implications for Design Creativity." *International Journal of Design* 1, no. 2 (2007): 21–33.

CASEL Briefs. *Background on Social and Emotional Learning (SEL)*. Chicago: University of Illinois, 2007.

Csibra, Gergely, and Gyorgy Gergely. "Social Learning and Social Cognition: The Case for Pedagogy." In *Processes of Change in Brain and Cognitive Development. Attention and Performance,* edited by Yuko Munakata and Mark Johnson, XXI. Oxford: Oxford University Press, 2006.

Edith, Grotberg, ed. *Resilience for Today: Gaining Strength from Adversity*. Westport: Praeger, 2003.

Engeström, Yrjö. *Learning by Expanding: An Activity Theoretical Approach to Developmental Research*. Helsinki: Orienta-Konsultit, 1987.

Engeström, Yrjö, Reijo Miettinen, and Raija-Leena Punamaki, eds. *Perspectives on Activity Theory*. Cambridge: Cambridge University Press, 1999.

Erdman, Jori, and Robert Weddle. "Designing/Building/Learning." *Journal of Architectural Education* 55, no. 3 (2002): 174–79.

Felsten, Gary, and Kathy Wilcox. "Influences of Stress and Situation-Specific Mastery Beliefs and Satisfaction with Social Support on Well-being and Academic Performance." *Psychological* Reports 70 (1992).

Folke, Carl. "Resilience (Republished)." *Ecology and Society* 21, no. 4 (2016).

Froud, Daisy, and Harriss Harriet, eds. *Radical Pedagogies: Architectural Education and the British Tradition*. London: RIBA Publishing, 2015.

Grotberg, Edith. "Countering Depression with the Five Building Blocks of Resilience." *Reaching Today's Youth* 4, no. 1 (1999).

Harriss, Harriet, and Lynette Wilder, eds. *Architecture Live Projects: Pedagogy into Practice*. New York: Routledge, 2014.

Howard-Jones, Paul. "Neuroscience and Education: Myths and Messages." *Nature Reviews Neuroscience* 15 (2014).

Hynes, William, Benjamin D. Trump, Alan Kirman, Andrew Haldane, and Igor Linkov. "Systemic Resilience in Economics." *Nature Physics* 18 (2022).

Irvine, William. *A Guide to the Good Life: The Ancient Art of Stoic Joy*. Oxford: Oxford University Press, 2009.

James, Mary, and Andrew Pollard. "TRLP's Ten Principles for Effective Pedagogy: Rationale, Development, Evidence, Argument and Impact." *Research Papers in Education* 26, no. 3 (2011).

Lave, Jean, and Etienne Wenger. *Situated Learning: Legitimate Peripheral Participation*. Cambridge: Cambridge University Press, 1991.

Lingard, Bob, Martin Mills, and Debra Hayes. "Teachers and Productive Pedagogies: Contextualising, Conceptualising, Utilising." *Pedagogy Culture and Society* 11, no. 3 (2003).

Luthar, Suniya, Dante Cicchetti, and Bronwyn Becker. "The Construct of Resilience: A Critical Evaluation and Guidelines for Future Work." *Child Development* 71, no. 3 (2000): 543–62.

Morrow, Ruth. "Creative Transformations." In *Design Studio Pedagogy: Horizons for the Future*, edited by Ashraf Salama and Nicholas Wilkinson, 100–14. Gateshead: The Urban International Press, 2007.

Morrow, Ruth, and James Benedict Brown. "Live Projects as Critical Pedagogies." In *Live Projects: Designing with People,* edited by Melanie Dodd, Fiona Harrisson, and Esther Charlesworth. Melbourne: RMIT Press, 2012.

National Trust. *National Trust Annual Report 20–21 [PDF]*. Swindon, UK: National Trust Publications, 2021. Accessed January 5, 2023.

Ng, Rashida. "What Will It Take? Reflections on Diversity, Equality and Inclusion in Architectural Education." *Journal of Architectural Education* 73, no. 2 (2019).

Resnick, Lauren, ed. *Knowing, Learning and Instruction: Essays in Honour of Robert Glaser*. Hillside NJ: Lawrence Erlbaum Associates, 1989.

Richardson, Glenn E. "The Metatheory of Resilience and Resiliency." *Journal of Clinical Psychology* 58, no. 3 (2002).

Salama, Ashraf. "A Theory for Integrating Knowledge in Architectural Design Education." *ArchNet-IJAR: International Journal of Architectural Research* 2, no. 1 (2008): 100–28.

Salama, Ashraf, and Michael J. Crosbie, eds. "Design Education: Explorations and Prospects for a Better Built Environment." *ArchNet-I-JAR: International Journal of Architectural Research* 4, no. 2–3 (2010): 1–466.

Schön, Donald. *The Design Studio: An Exploration of Its Traditions and Potentials*. London: RIBA Publications, 1985.

Smith, Carl A., and Mark E. Boyer. "Adapted Verbal Feedback, Instructor Interaction of Student Emotions in the Landscape Architecture Studio." *International Journal of Art and Design Education* 34, no. 2 (2015).

Ungar, Michael. "Systemic Resilience: Principles and Processes for a Science of Change in Contexts of Adversity." *Ecology and Society* 23, no. 4 (2018).

Watt, Kathleen, and Derek Cottrell. "Grounding the Curriculum: Learning from Live Projects in Architectural Education." *International Journal of Learning* 13 (2006): 97–104.

Youdell, Deborah. "Bioscience and the Sociology of Education: The Case for Biosocial Education." *British Journal of Sociology of Education* 38, no. 8 (2017).

Youdell, Deborah, and Martin R. Lindley. *Biosocial Education: The Social and Biological Entanglements of Learning*. New York: Routledge, 2018.

Zedner, Moshe, and Endler Norman, eds. *Handbook of Coping: Theory, Research, Applications*. New York: John Wiley and Sons, 1996.

4 Adapting Practice-Based Learning in Transdisciplinary Teams to Enhance Student Success Skills

Aziza Cyamani, Charles Chioma Nwaizu and Noor Al Maamari

Introduction

In today's ever-changing professional landscape, employers are increasingly desiring graduates with competencies that transcend disciplinary boundaries, including success skills in collaboration, communication and critical thinking.[1] Scriven and Paul comprehensively define critical thinking as "the intellectually disciplined process of actively and skillfully conceptualizing, applying, analyzing, synthesizing, and/or evaluating information gathered from, or generated by observation, experience, reflection, reasoning, or communication, as a guide to belief and action".[2] Cummings also pointed to the use of language as "in the service of thinking and problem solving".[3] To bring these faculties into the classroom, Student Success Skills (SSS), also known as 21st Century Competencies,[4] are defined as cognitive, personal and professional competencies associated with and contributing to students' developmental success during and beyond their academic careers. These skills include, but are not limited to, higher-order thinking skills, such as critical thinking, problem-solving, decision-making and creative thinking;[5] and personal skills such as intrapersonal skills (e.g., work ethic, self-reflection and evaluation, flexibility, adaptability), and interpersonal skills (e.g., teamwork, collaboration, communication and leadership). Tied together, the development of cognitive processes with social aptitudes are linked to improved academic and professional performance.

In the pilot study presented in this chapter, students were immersed in a practice-based learning project, which began with an open-ended, authentic (i.e., real-world) problem. To this effect, and with the help of external partners, the teaching team introduced the problem through lectures and secondary information. Students were then assigned to work collaboratively in groups to further their understanding of the problem, define their own direction, and offer solution(s) to the problem in transdisciplinary teams. Transdisciplinary teams in this context were defined as a learning environment involving students from different disciplines and external partners working alongside one another to solve a real-world problem: mitigating postharvest loss in Nigeria.

DOI: 10.4324/9781032705927-5

Establishing the Problem Context

Currently, our socio-ecological system is unsustainable, as we are facing global challenges pertaining to the environment, socio-politics and the economy, including climate change, scarce natural resources, poverty and other contemporary issues.[6] These challenges have been summarized through the United Nations' 17 Sustainable Development Goals (SDG). More specifically, SDG 12 "Responsible Consumption and Production" was identified among the greatest global challenges. With the human population estimated to reach 9.7 billion in 2050, and food requirements estimated to be 70% higher than today,[7] addressing this challenge requires not only increased food production, but also strategies to reduce postharvest loss and food waste, which has been recognized as vital for meeting global food and energy needs.[8] Critically, these solutions will require an exceptionally creative and prepared next-generation workforce collaborating across all areas of expertise to achieve sustainable change.

Cultivation of fruits, as a microcosm of these food challenges, exemplify the complexities within our socio-ecological system. In particular, the role that tomatoes play beyond meeting dietary requirements. Their cultivation contributes to boosting the economy of developing nations by fostering trade, generating income and creating steady employment. In Nigeria, the second largest producer of fresh tomatoes in Africa and 16th largest tomato producer globally, the tomato industry is substantial. However, challenges within the tomato value chain compounded by the susceptibility of tomatoes to damage, lead to considerable postharvest losses of approximately 45% in Nigeria.[9] These challenges underscore the pressing need for innovative and sustainable solutions to ensure resilience of the global food systems.

Design for Sustainability and Design at the Base of the Pyramid

The contribution of design towards a just, healthy and prosperous world has been recognized since the 20th century. Designers are seen as influencing the way products are made, used and discarded. They are involved in the decisions of selecting materials, production methods, finishes and packaging methods for products that impact the environment.[10] Although sustainability lacks a commonly accepted definition, literature has shown that our theoretical understanding of the concept continues to evolve. Successful undertakings are credited to be shifting from outcomes-based approaches to systems-based approaches that prioritize processes, multiple scales, systematic thinking and which are ultimately guided by a clear vision.[11] In line with this evolution, the design philosophies within which sustainability is considered have evolved as well, from green design to ecodesign to design for sustainability.[12] The last, which is the subject of this study and commonly abbreviated as DFS, is seen as the broader, more complex definition accounting for more radical innovations in product, service and system schemes, questioning the function at all stages of the product life cycle and influencing existing patterns of consumption.[13]

Design at the Base of the Pyramid (DBoP) is one such DFS philosophy that addresses the challenges and opportunities in creating innovative solutions for communities living in lower income brackets, often referred to as the "Base of the Pyramid" (BoP). Recognizing the financial constraints faced at the BoP, this philosophy aims to apply design thinking to develop solutions that are economically feasible, ethically responsible and environmentally sustainable, thereby improving BoP living conditions. Santos, Krämer and Vezzoli emphasize this strategy's holistic and sustainable approach as transcending mere low-cost alternatives of product design.[14] Rather, designers practicing DBoP aim to create products and services that meet the community's needs while considering wider societal, environmental and economic impacts aligning with the triple bottom line sustainability concept. Castillo delves deeper into DBoP, highlighting the importance of local engagement and contextual awareness and crediting successful design as involving immersion in cultural and socioeconomic contexts and active community involvement in co-creation.[15] Empowerment is central to DBoP, granting BoP communities the agency to devise solutions tailored to their unique challenges and aspirations.

Pedagogical Approach

Teaching approaches are evolving to integrate cognitive, personal and professional skills as instructors seek to instill deeper learning competencies in their students. These skills encompass essential competencies that transcend disciplinary boundaries and are highly valued in the professional world due to their associations with both immediate and long-term outcomes.[16] Active learning, among other teaching approaches, is one method employed to foster the development of these skills.[17] It emphasizes student engagement with course materials using active methods such as dialogue, discussions, debate, writing, group work, role-playing and/or problem-solving. Active learning as defined by Bonwell and Eison involves instructional activities that engage students in doing things and thinking about what they are doing, fostering higher-order thinking and the construction of knowledge and understanding.[18] Constructivist learning theory, as developed by Piaget and Vygotsky, serves as the theoretical foundation for active learning, underscoring that learners construct knowledge by actively building connections between new information and their existing knowledge and experiences.[19]

A meta-analysis of 225 research studies on STEM education carried out by Freeman et al. found that in comparison to conventional, lecture-based training, active learning considerably improves students' performance. As defined in this study, active learning entails instructional practices where students engage in tasks such as problem-solving, peer instruction and group discussions to encourage critical thinking. The findings showed that students in contexts with active learning not only had greater exam scores by half a standard deviation, but also lower failure rates of 21.8% compared with traditional lecturing rates of 33.8%.[20] The results were consistent across all STEM disciples, and highlight the transformative potential of active learning in enhancing learning outcomes and encouraging student involvement in STEM education, positioning it as a critical tactic for preparing students for the challenges of the 21st century.

Active learning methodologies align with these constructivist principles, as they require students to make these vital connections through various interactive processes. Metacognition, or students' reflection on their own learning processes, plays a pivotal role in constructivist learning theory and is central to the active learning experience. In the realm of educational methodologies, two distinct approaches, project-based learning (PjBL) and problem-based learning (PBL), play a pivotal role in fostering success skills. While they are both student-centered learning strategies that aim at fostering deeper learning through active exploration of real-world problems, they are often designed using case studies to frame real-life problems. The challenge with using case studies is that they look at the past rather than towards the future, and are subject to the limitations and biases of the instructor who develops them. Also, through case studies, the instructor sets specific boundaries for the problem, making it more manageable within the course and program constraints. While this controlled approach helps with practical reasons, it limits students' engagement and understanding of complexity.

Practice-based learning (PRBL) provides such opportunities, where students can engage with open-ended, unbounded, unscoped authentic problems. Within this learning approach, students can self-direct their learning process through problem-solving methods akin to professional practice and within learning environments closely mirroring real-world settings. This approach emphasizes hands-on experiences and assessments aimed at evaluating competency. PRBL strategies are believed to enhance students' understanding by requiring them to engage in critical analysis to derive knowledge, meaning and insight from real-life experiences. Practice-based learning (PRBL) introduces students to real-world challenges at the outset of the educational process, nurturing critical thinking, problem-solving and the application of knowledge. The curriculum in PRBL is structured around addressing contextual challenges, and assessments are tailored to measure students' problem-solving proficiency.

Various frameworks of practice-based learning have been developed to boost teaching effectiveness and consequently improve success skills.[21] MacLaughlan and Lodge employed practice-based learning using a cognitive apprenticeship model that requires a design-based solution to a real-life problem.[22]

Anvik et al. also incorporated practice-based learning in a nursing home to study the interplay between formal and informal learning situations,[23] while Hollis and Eren incorporated real-world industrial case studies into a food science course to improve student success skills.[24] Matzembacher et al. studied the impacts of a practice-based learning methodology that involves the provision of community services on students' engagement and learning perception,[25] and Mann et al. presented a framework for practice-based education in engineering as an alternative approach that lifts learners out of traditional structures and repositions them within an authentic professional practice.[26] In their study, students were challenged to solve real problems and offer service to the community as if they were experts. Their results revealed that practice-based methodology led students to greater engagement. Such practice-based learning emulates real-world industry practices, hence illustrating higher education best practices.[27]

Though PRBL outcomes can be unpredictable, preliminary evidence demonstrates that it allows students to practice technical and personal skills, including critical analysis and synthesis of information, realizing and assessing solutions, teamwork, communication and organization. Most precedents employing PRBL involved an instructor guiding interdisciplinary student teams to proffer solutions to identified, scoped and/or designed projects that mimic or streamline the real problem into a manageable scope. The instructor's ability to frame complex problems into manageable parts is a practical way to expose students to a practice-based learning environment without causing confusion. This combined evidence strongly supports the need for a comprehensive and collaborative approach when applying practice-based learning to address real-life challenges.

By situating a DBoP topic in an applicable social-economic community such as Nigeria, which experiences tomato postharvest loss, the project in this chapter embodied learning objectives that offered students the opportunity to engage in practice-based learning, transdisciplinary collaboration, cross-cultural knowledge transfer and exposure to a global vision of sustainability.

Methodology

The inception of the class project emerged from a discussion about tomato postharvest loss in Africa between two faculty members at the University of Nebraska-Lincoln. This conversation eventually led to the pivotal question: Have you considered approaching the issue from a design perspective? Buchanan explains this confluence of disciplines well when he described design functioning as an integrative discipline because it has no subject matter of its own. Rather, it formulates quasi-subject matter from an indeterminate subject waiting to be made specifically concrete.[28]

Recognizing that the problem of food loss, particularly postharvest loss, was a complex and multifaceted issue that could be a wicked problem,[29] the teaching team set out to design a student project prompt that leveraged patterns of reasoning employed in design thinking and systems thinking to address a societal problem rooted in food science and sustainability. A crucial element of the project was to anchor the problem within a community that not only experiences the problem but has received limited attention in terms of solutions. Consequently, Nigeria was selected as the focus of the study, a choice facilitated by one of the faculty members having already conducted research in the region and established a network of local partners, as it was imperative that the local community play a role in the process to limit bias and unintended consequences. While projects of this nature might appear commonplace, multidisciplinary collaborative efforts involving community partners are relatively sparse in higher education. Rowe highlighted the significance of these pedagogical approaches when he argued that for graduates to make meaningful contributions in addressing society's most complex problems, they needed to be exposed as students to such issues in higher education, and through innovative pedagogical approaches, build capacity to turn knowledge into action.[30]

The overarching goal of this study was to identify how practice-based learning (PRBL) approaches within transdisciplinary teams could enhance students' success skills, specifically focusing on critical thinking, communication and collaboration skills. The objective was to integrate design and systems thinking, along with scientific approaches to examine and propose solutions for mitigating tomato postharvest loss in Nigeria. The research design employed mixed methods in collecting quantitative data using a critical thinking rubric, and qualitative data using a questionnaire with close-ended and open-ended questions. This method was chosen because of the small sample size in the classroom, which limited generalizability but provided opportunities for contextualization. Both quantitative and qualitative data were collected at the same time, and analysis and interpretation were based on convergent parallels drawn between both sets of results.

Pre-Planning: Collaboration Across Disciplines

This study involved students enrolled in a food processing course (FDST 420 – Fruit and Vegetable Processing Technology) and Contemporary Issues in Product Design (IDES 491 – Special Topics) at the University of Nebraska-Lincoln. FDST 420 covered the fundamentals of harvesting and postharvest handling (storage, processing, packaging) of fruit and vegetables and the necessary control strategies to mitigate safety and quality changes that can reduce the storage life of the product and result in postharvest losses. The course introduced students to primary strategies for addressing the technical aspects of fruits and vegetables with specific reference to harvesting, storage, processing, packaging and transportation, along with storage-life-increasing technologies that minimized postharvest loss. The second course, IDES-491 was a professional elective in the minor program of Product Design housed in the Department of Interior Design that covered the identification of contemporary design opportunities, analysis of impacts of products through a sustainability lens and implementation of design practices that create positive, ethical, social and environmental impacts. Specifically, this course explored practical projects on DFS and DBoP. Students enrolled in IDES 491 included five undergraduate and one graduate student, and their major areas of study included interior design, architecture and mechanical engineering.

Planning for the project began with the exercise of aligning course work and calendars between the two courses to create an opportunity for synchronized collaboration. The project was scheduled for the last month of the semester to give students the opportunity to gain theoretical grounding in the topics in their respective courses while preparing for the collaborative project. Due to differing class meeting times, the project was conducted using both remote and in-person meeting platforms to accommodate external partners, as well as minimize disrution to students' already established schedules.

Project Programming

A month-long collaborative project between the two courses was developed based on the real-life problem of food loss in Nigeria. The project entailed students in both courses working alongside one another with the knowledge support of external partners to form transdisciplinary teams. External partners included government policymakers and practitioners. Two transdisciplinary teams composed of one student from FDST 420 and two students from IDES 491 were each involved in this month-long pilot study. In addition, two different external partners (one government policymaker and one postharvest consultant) consulted with the teams throughout the project. In total, six students ($N = 6$) took part in this study. All students gave their consent to participate in the study, which was approved by the human subjects institutional research board (IRB) at UNL.

In defining the scope of this project, the teaching team considered the project schedule, contextual aspects and the students' practical design skills. Due to these practicalities, the instructors decided to limit the final deliverable to a conceptual solution. A conceptual solution is commonly recognized as the foundation upon which the final product is built and acts as a roadmap towards the development of the final solution, explicitly embodying the goal of the project, and to some degree, defining the form and technical considerations of the product's architecture. Furthermore, the objectives of the project could be achieved within this framework. The project entailed three phases: 1) Information Gathering; 2) Solution Finding; and 3) Solution Assessment.

Phase 1: During the first phase, students were introduced to the problem with the help of external partners, followed by lectures on the theory of DBoP and food postharvest loss. After this initial introduction, students were charged with conducting their own research focusing on seven topics: people, community, environment, products, materials, technology, and fruit (tomatoes). Each group researched three topics, in addition to fruit. This first phase culminated in preliminary research presentations, synthesis of their findings and framing of design problems using the "*How Might We . . .*" design thinking premise intended to elicit creative ideas. The groups also defined a set actionable criterion to guide the solution finding phase. This process, while challenging for students, is critical in stimulating a problem-solving attitude, as it establishes ownership of the problem in the practice-based project. It was vital to the project that the problem be introduced with enough information to familiarize students with the problem without inhibiting their ability for discovery. Through engaging in active learning methods such as conducting their own research via external partner consultations, literature review and working collaboratively, students thus discovered more insights about the topic.

Phase 2: Moving into the second phase of the project, students worked in groups to ideate possible solutions to the problem. At this stage, the faculty acted as facilitators rather than instructors to allow students to leverage a multidisciplinary range of knowledge and skills to come up with suitable, sustainable solutions. During consultations with students, the teaching team asked probing questions to encourage reasoned decisions and ensure that the design proposals met the project's objectives. Midway through this second phase, each group presented at least two different ideas of possible solutions to external partners and received feedback on the most viable solutions. Feedback included design development considerations, such as material selection, local fabrication and production capabilities, market considerations and infrastructure. This was a turning point in the project, as from this point, the chosen idea would then be developed to the conceptual level. Students spent the rest of the time in this phase refining the conceptual solution and producing presentation materials. At the end of the solution finding phase, each group presented visual assets of their concept to a juried panel that included the teaching team, external partners from Nigeria (who joined the class remotely) and their peers.

Phase 3: After completing the design process, students were tasked with writing individual reports that critically analyzed, synthesized and evaluated their conceived conceptual solution(s) to the problem. By engaging in this critical report assignment, students were encouraged to explain their own thinking processes, evaluate their proposed solution(s) to the tomato postharvest loss problem in Nigeria and justify the decisions inferred in their solution(s). These reflective reports provided insight into the group's reasoned decisions and discernment between group and individual thinking systems.

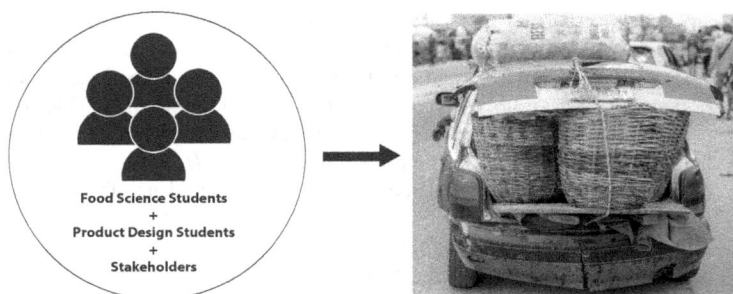

Figure 4.1 Schematic representation of the teaching methodology. Illustration by authors. Photograph by Tolu Owoeye/Shutterstock.com

Student Project

The transdisciplinary teams identified that most of the postharvest loss in the tomato value chain occurred during transportation (see Figure 4.1), typically from farms located in the northern part of Nigeria to markets in Lagos, in the southern part of Nigeria. Findings indicated that tomatoes were sensitive to external forces, resulting in puncturing, pressure and bruising. Moreover, their perishability was caused by their respiration and transpiration rates and the relative humidity and temperature in which they were stored. Tomatoes are a climacteric fruit and consistently release ethylene gas, making them prone to spoiling due to their high-water content. These factors were found to contribute to the high losses incurred after harvesting tomatoes in Nigeria, along with changes in environmental, climatic, economic and political conditions. Other issues identified included mishandling of tomatoes during harvest, inefficient packaging and transportation methods that relied on unrefrigerated trucks and bikes. These factors led to reduction in freshness and quality and negatively impacted the value of tomatoes by the time they reached the market. It was concluded that Nigerian farmers and stakeholders needed more efficient and safer methods of transporting commercial tomatoes to mitigate postharvest loss.

After Phase 1 – discovery phase, one of the transdisciplinary teams reframed the design problem as follows: *How might we design a solution to postharvest loss due to incompetent securing methods to motor vehicles?* Insights derived from their research highlighted the following criteria that a successful design within the scope of the reframed question should adhere to

- Easily carried to and from markets and farms (strap and flat-pack design)
- Stackable for vehicle transport
- Smooth interior (tomato protection)
- Rounded edges (human comfort)

- Reusable (Affordability)
- Sustainability (repurposed materials)

The team conceptualized a new packaging and storage solution designed to reduce tomato postharvest loss during short and long-distance transportation without relying on refrigeration. The designed container and storage unit addressed challenges in transportation while maintaining freshness of the tomato fruits through form and structural considerations. It incorporated features such as stacking ability, accommodation of different transportation methods, ventilation and minimizing compression.

The conceptual design included distinctive elements such as a hexagonal shape, operable hinges, slots for ventilation and inside dividers as illustrated in Figures 4.2a and 4.2b. The dividers were strategically incorporated to limit layers of tomatoes stacked together in a single chamber to minimize pressure caused by overpacking, enhance transpiration and consequently slow down ripening and softening of the tomatoes. The container unit was envisioned as being constructed using plastic material for durability and weight efficiency. Specifically, the team proposed the use of recycled plastic for sustainability.

Two auxiliary design interventions were proposed along with the container and storage unit: (1) That farmers could sun dry a portion of the tomatoes harvested, and (2) That the container and storage unit could be designed to be flat-packed and feature graphics on the interior surface with visual assembly and customization instructions. The design exercise was concluded at this conceptual stage, and a basic comparative analysis using a customized LiDS wheel[31] methodology was conducted. As shown in Figure 4.2c, the analysis revealed perceived advantages of the container compared to the currently used raffia baskets. Students identified improvements to be in certain areas of the container such as enhanced ventilation, increased container durability, enhanced food safety and better fulfillment of packaging and storage needs. The new conceptualized solution was generally deemed to have a favorable effect on reducing tomato postharvest loss during transportation.

Data Collection and Analysis

Quantitative data was collected using an analytical rubric adapted from a critical thinking measurement rubric developed by the Center for Teaching, Learning, & Technology at Washington State University.[32] The rubric evaluated five assessment criteria, which included students' ability to (1) Summarize the problem, (2) Consider context and assumptions, (3) Communicate their own perspective, or position, (4) Assess conclusions, implications, and consequences, and (5) Communicate effectively. The rubric scored each assessment criteria individually using a numerical score representing the degree to which a student met each criterion. The three levels of achievement were "emerging", "developing", and "mastering". To score the reports with

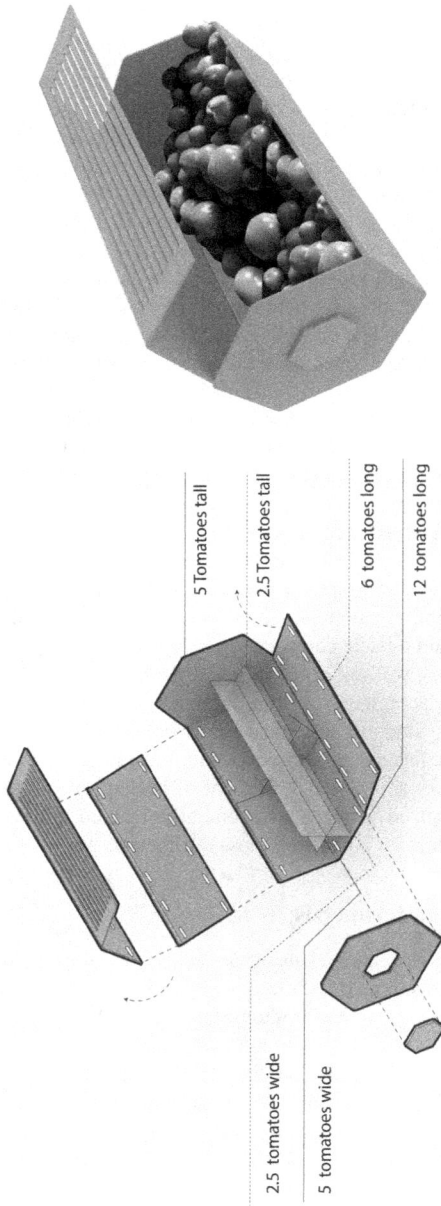

5 Tomatoes tall

2.5 Tomatoes tall

6 tomatoes long

12 tomatoes long

2.5 tomatoes wide

5 tomatoes wide

Figure 4.2a Hexagonal tomato container. Illustration by students

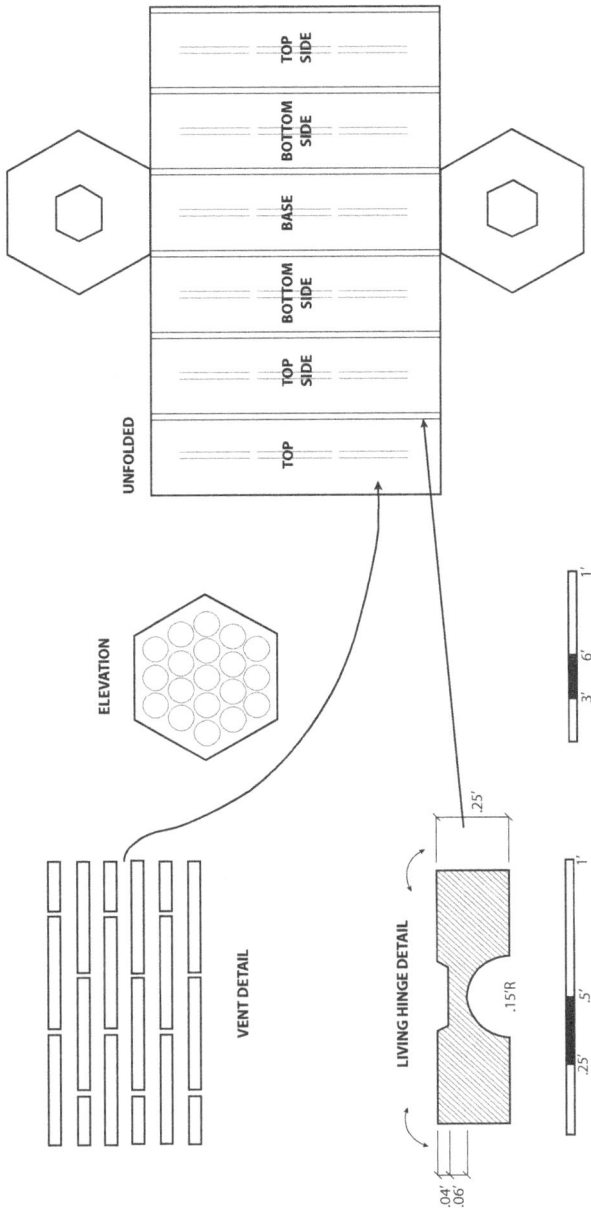

Figure 4.2b Construction of the hexagonal tomato container. Illustration by students

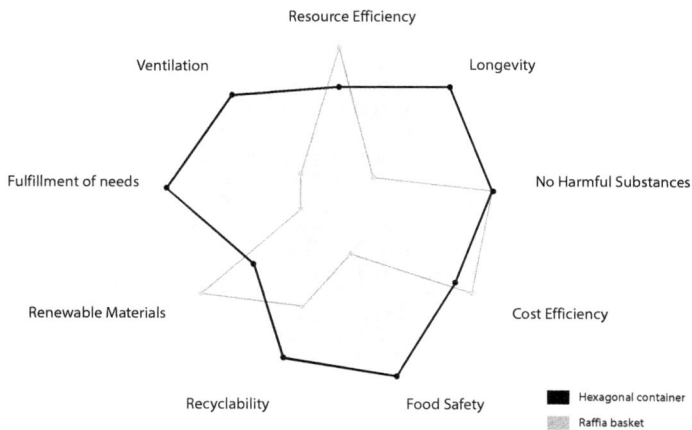

Figure 4.2c A LiDS wheel benchmarking improvements in hexagonal tomato container compared to the traditional raffia basket. Illustration by students

the rubric, three different reviewers including the instructors independently rated the students' reports. Each reviewer was trained in the use of the assessment rubric before the actual student reports from the study were judged. The average scores from the three raters were then used in the study.

Fundamental quantitative analysis was employed to assess the scores reflecting students' critical thinking levels. Using averages, most students demonstrated developing levels of critical thinking. As illustrated in Figure 4.3, the distribution of average total scores indicates that four students, or 66.67% of the participants, scored within the developing level, while one student, or 16.67% of the participants, scored at the emerging and mastering levels, each.

Moreover, a questionnaire featuring both close-ended and open-ended questions was designed and administered remotely after Phase 3. The tool aimed to capture students' perceptions of critical thinking and the DBoP project, as well as gain insights into students' perceptions on collaboration and communication within transdisciplinary teams. All six students responded to the questionnaire, resulting in a response rate of 100%. Close-ended questions prompted students to rate their experiences using 4-Point Likert Items (Strongly Disagree, Disagree, Agree and Strongly Agree), while open-ended questions asked students to elaborate on these experiences. The following questions were posed:

Preliminary analysis of the questionnaire revealed patterns in students' perceptions of engaging in an active learning and transdisciplinary collaborative project. No broad inferences were drawn from the Likert items due to the limited sample size. However, when combined with the open-ended

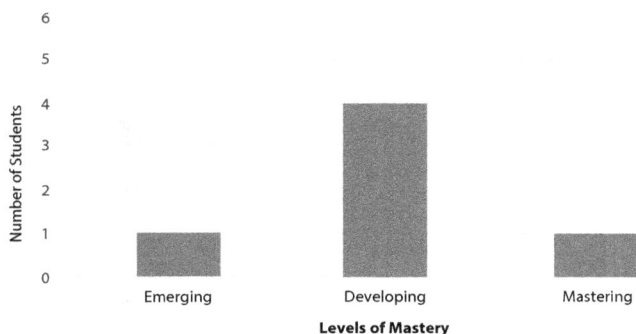

Figure 4.3 Mastery of critical thinking in transdisciplinary teams

questions, a more comprehensive understanding of students' perspectives was achieved. As shown in Figure 4.4a, in response to critical thinking, all students strongly agreed that the project provided them with the opportunity to critically think about proposing solution(s) to prevent and/or mitigate postharvest loss of tomatoes. When asked about the challenges they faced in defining the problem, students pointed to various difficulties, including gathering information, distilling initial data, analyzing the nuances of the problem, choosing an area to focus on, understanding the Nigerian context and working around the environmental and technical limitations of the region.

Regarding the methods that were helpful in conceiving a solution, students referenced the firsthand information they received from partners, in-class lectures and information from secondary sources such as websites and published literature. When asked about assumptions, most students pointed to their limited knowledge about Nigeria. One student wrote,

One assumption I made on this project was the thought process that we couldn't find a solution with the little resources that Nigeria has, because of the very fragile nature of tomatoes and just spoilable produce itself. However, my assumption changed as we started to learn more about their current methods of transportation of the tomatoes, and how they can be improved with resources that they would be able to get affordably.

In terms of collaboration, most students mentioned that they preferred working in multidisciplinary teams rather than interdisciplinary teams, as shown in Figure 4.4b. Additionally, the majority of students strongly rated their participation in team decisions and conclusions as adequate. When asked

Table 4.1 Questionnaire

Topics	Likert Items	Open-Ended Questions
Critical Thinking	1. The project provided me with the opportunity to critically think on how to propose solution(s) to prevent and/or mitigate post-harvest loss of tomatoes.	2. In defining the problem, what did you find challenging? 3. What methods were helpful in finding a solution to the problem? What information did you feel was missing? 4. What assumptions did you have before or while working on the project? How did they change?
Collaboration	5. I prefer to work in a team that involves multidisciplinary collaboration than working in teams with members from my discipline only. 6. I was able to adequately participate in my team's project decisions and conclusions.	7. What do you believe were the strengths and weaknesses of your multidisciplinary team?
Communication	8. The project provided me with the opportunity to improve my presentation and communication skills through the interactive sessions organized during the project.	
Project	9. I was exposed to a real-life (global) challenge on food loss and food security issues. 10. The objectives of the project were clearly defined.	11. What did you find challenging in this project? What did you find helpful in this project? 12. In what ways can we improve the project?

about the strengths of their teams, students pointed to the benefit of having diversified knowledge, skills and perspectives. They emphasized the catalytic effect of this diversity on generating different ideas (i.e., thinking outside the box) and validating decisions. This latter point was further attributed to having team members who were well-versed in scientific knowledge regarding tomatoes. One student mentioned that

it was a strength to have a team member who knew how and what to research when it came to the tomato fruit. Usually, it takes twice as

Q1: The project provided me with the opportunity to critically think on how to propose solution(s) to prevent and/or mitigate post-harvest loss of tomatoes.

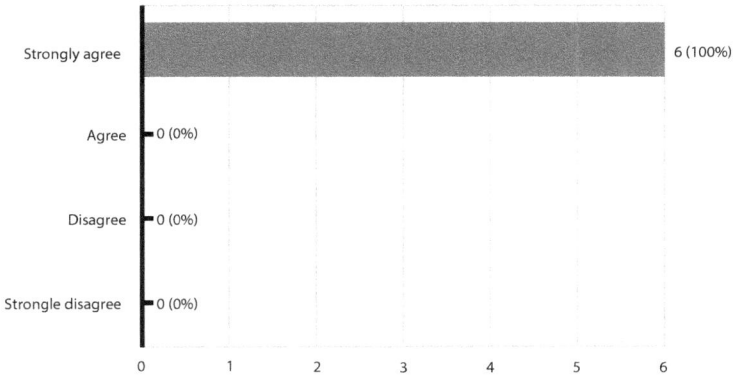

Figure 4.4a Students' perceptions of critical thinking

long for design students to learn how to search for the answer and what questions to ask. It definitely cut our research in half and made it more effective.

Students also identified weaknesses in the project such as conflicting schedules and concerns about group size. They expressed a desire to form larger groups and emphasized the need to devise mechanisms to keep all students engaged at every stage of the project, particularly during design development.

Similarly, the majority of students agreed that the project provided them an opportunity to enhance their presentation and communication skills, as shown in Figure 4.4c. This perception can be attributed to the number of presentations built into the project and direct communication with external partners. It was observed during the project that students' ability to interact with external partners improved throughout the project.

Regarding students' perceptions of the overall project, as shown in Figure 4.4d, the majority of students concurred that the project objectives were met and that the project exposed them to a real-life challenge. Suggestions for improving the project focused primarily on logistical aspects such as the time commitment of completing the project alongside other classes, the project's duration, schedule conflicts among team members and technical and connectivity challenges while communicating with partners. Another significant issue was the involvement of non-design students in design-based workflows. Some students expressed the challenge of being unfamiliar with the design process, leading to uncertainties about their contribution to design

Q6: I was able to adequately participate in my team's project decisions and conclusions.

Q5: I prefer to work in a team that involves multidisciplinary collaboration than working in teams with members from my discipline only.

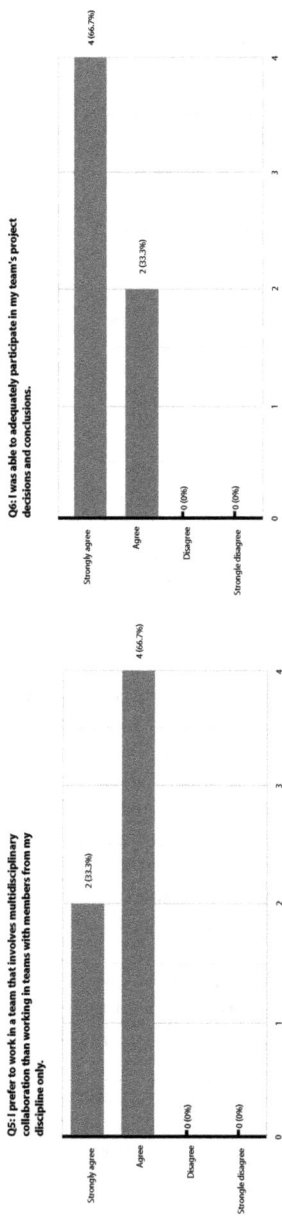

Figure 4.4b Students' perceptions of collaboration

Q8: The project provided me with the opportunity to improve my presentation and communication skills through the interactive sessions organized during the project.

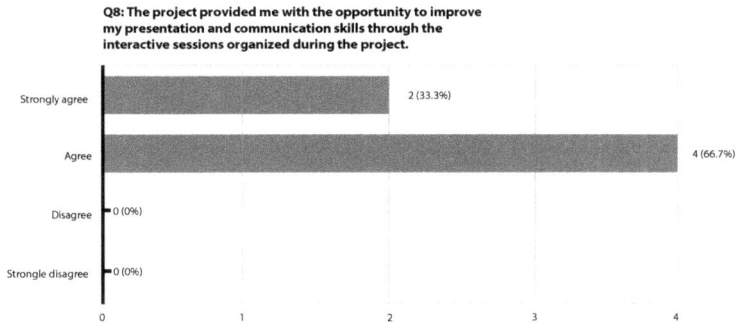

Figure 4.4c Students' perceptions of communication

development. Suggestions for enhancing the project included a desire to increase stakeholder participation at every stage of the process.

While the student conceptual solution presented earlier showed viable considerations for mitigating tomato postharvest loss during transportation, it still presented areas that required further development. The external partners expressed concerns about these aspects during student presentations, and students reflected on them in their critical analysis. The partners indicated that the container's adaptability could be hindered by its cost due to the chosen materials and manufacturing needs. They inferred that the average tomato farmer in Nigeria might not be able to afford it and touched on the implications of limited local plastic manufacturing capabilities and the environmental impacts of plastic, even though the team had suggested the use of recycled materials from the community. To this end, one student reflected on the possibility of first establishing a system of plastic collection, recycling and production, which could in the long run offset the price of the containers. The external partners also pointed out that the reduced capacity of the new containers compared to the raffia baskets could impact farmers' and marketers' preference.

In their reflections, students contended that transportation methods that ensured the delivery of higher-quality tomatoes to markets justified a potential reduction in quantity. This was a point that required further studies to understand Nigerian farmers and marketers' perceptions. Students also mentioned that strong community advocacy would need to be integrated into the solution to ensure local buy-in, especially as the benefits of using the improved packaging and storage unit might not be immediate. All students expressed the necessity for prototyping, testing and evaluating the technical aspects of the container and storage unit.

This preliminary data unveiled opportunities for conducting more in-depth comparative studies on changes in students' success skills in relation to both active learning approaches and topics exploring design at the base of the pyramid.

Q10: The objectives of the project were clearly defined.

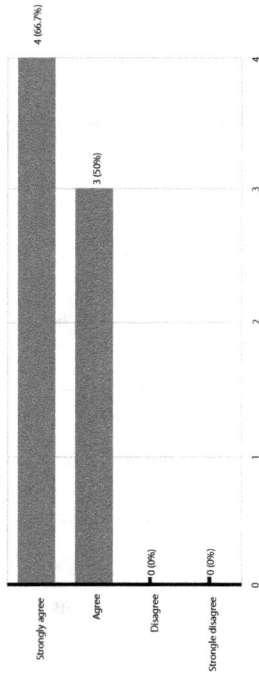

Q9: I was exposed to a real-life (global) challenge on food loss and food security issues.

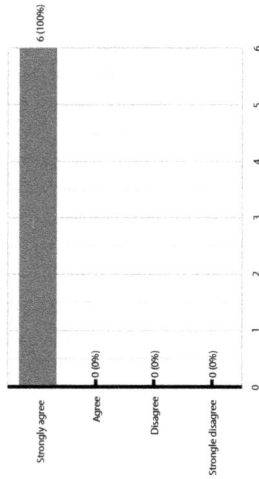

Figure 4.4d Students' perceptions of the overall project

Discussion

This study investigated how active learning approaches, particularly practice-based learning (PRBL) in transdisciplinary teams enhanced students' success skills – specifically, critical thinking, communication and collaboration. Students in this study demonstrated a range of performance levels in critical thinking from developing to mastery. They exhibited what Facione referred to as a critical spirit, characterized by probing inquisitiveness and eagerness for reliable information.[5] Students' ability to articulate the "why" (explanation) of decisions, inferred from interpretating information about an unfamiliar place and the prosing possible solutions, reflected the positive impact of practice-based learning on enhancing these skills. This outcome aligned with other studies across various education settings and programs.[33] Furthermore, the use of reflective reports within the critical thinking process emerged as a powerful tool in nurturing students' abilities in constructing pervasive arguments. This approach showcased the potential for students to integrate feedback, data and evidence from their transdisciplinary teams into their own reasoning and decision-making processes. According to Quitadamo and Kurtz, writing scientific arguments is a multifaceted task that requires the application of various cognitive skills, including critical thinking, problem-solving and analytical thinking.[34] By employing individual reports, students honed these skills and improved their overall critical thinking abilities. The following were the main observations in critical thinking that were observed in the student reports, including enhanced students' systems thinking mindsets, problem-solving skills and contextual and cultural sensitivities.

Systems Thinking Mindset

All of the students' individual reports indicated a shift in their perception of the problem and, consequently, the solution. They exhibited understanding of the intricate interconnections that existed among various facets of the problem, including the fruit itself, farmers, transportation methods, government and markets in their analysis. They embraced the complexity of the issue, conducted thorough examination of the tomato value chain and identified areas of intervention. Furthermore, they recognized the multitude of perspectives from which a solution could be conceived. For instance, one student mentioned that while the tomato postharvest issue could be addressed in many ways, focusing on transportation from a product design perspective made the most sense. Another student articulated that transportation was selected because it was the phase in the tomato value chain where most tomatoes perished.

Additionally, students delved into the use of recycled plastic and the necessity of establishing a complimentary system to facilitate the process of collecting, recycling and manufacturing the plastic container. In support of their choice of materials, they conducted research and identified specific companies in Nigeria with the capability to fabricate plastic containers. It is important to highlight the role of engaging with external partners throughout different stages of the design process: for instance, in response to the proposed recycling system, the partners emphasized that establishing such a process would take a long time and that local capabilities at the time were neither organized nor easily accessible to facilitate this process. This engagement with external partners enriched the students' learning experience and added depth and validation to the project.

Problem-Solving

The adoption of a problem-solving mindset was another pattern observed in the students' analysis. Students thoughtfully considered both the larger and smaller decisions made throughout the project. Firstly, they reflected on the overall design of the concept, recognizing its merits in aligning with the goals and criteria set forth in their design statement. During the iterative process, the conceptual solution evolved through a series of developments as students made decisions on specific aspects, all while considering the broader system. For instance, one student raised concerns about how the use of plastic might affect local raffia weavers' employment opportunities. In the design process, the role of the teaching team shifted from instructors to facilitators who asked probing questions. This interactive exchange enabled students to maintain full ownership of the conceptualized solution while honing their critical thinking skills.

Contextual and Cultural Sensitivity

All students on the team demonstrated critical discourse by acknowledging the limitation of their knowledge regarding the Nigerian context. They recognized that making assumptions about Nigeria was inevitable since they had never visited the country. To address this, they emphasized the necessity of further developing the conceptual solution and conducting tests related to storage, tomato ripening, ventilation and stacking to assess its suitability for Nigeria. Students expressed the benefits of collaborating with external partners with whom they could directly engage to fill in contextual gaps, which in turn helped them to develop valuable skills in communicating with partners from a different cultural background. They also expressed appreciation for gaining a deeper understanding of the Nigerian community and addressing a real-life issue.

Conclusion

In conclusion, this pilot study demonstrated the potential of employing practice-based learning methods to enhance student success skills. By offering this project using the "learn by doing" approach, we observed a notable increase in students' enthusiasm for problem-solving, critical thinking, collaboration, and creativity. Furthermore, this study underscored opportunities to enhance students' proficiency in a variety of skills (practical, soft and knowledge-based) through collaborative efforts and cross-disciplinary interactions. The project's practical and real-life characteristics, coupled with the valuable input from external partners, resulted in heightened student engagement and a strengthened sense of ownership of the design process. Preliminary data revealed that students gained awareness of the intricacies of the tomato value chain industry in Nigeria, and a broader understanding of the systematic challenges related to responsible consumption and production.

This project also highlighted the significance of design in bridging cultural barriers. It provided students with the opportunity to address a broad sustainability problem focusing on communities living at the base of the pyramid. Through this process, the results demonstrated how thoughtful design thinking processes can contribute to successful transdisciplinary collaboration and create effective solutions with underserved populations.

Given the positive outcomes of this study, our teaching team is actively exploring additional avenues of collaboration to better prepare the next generation of critical thinkers. We are exploring the impacts of real-world projects, especially those at the base of the pyramid and collaborations across disciplines on developing students' sustainability competencies. We are committed to continuing to facilitate opportunities that empower students to apply their knowledge in practical and meaningful ways that foster the development of well-rounded, solution-oriented and workforce-ready graduates.

Notes

1 Slalana Živkoviɫ, "A Model of Critical Thinking as an Important Attribute for Success in the 21st Century," *Procedia-Social and Behavioral Sciences* 232 (2016): 102–8; Francine H. Hollis and Fulya Eren, "Implementation of Real-world Experiential Learning in a Food Science Course Using a Food Industry-Integrated Approach," *Journal of Food Science Education* 15, no. 4 (2016): 109–19.

2 Scriven Michael and Richard Paul, "Defining Critical Thinking," Statement by Micheal Scriven and Richard Paul in *8th Annual International Conference on Critical Thinking and Education Reform*, Summer 1987. http://www.criticalthinking.org/pages/defining-critical-thinking/766

3 Jim Cummins, "Age on Arrival and Immigrant Second Language Learning in Canada: A Reassessment1," *Applied Linguistics* 2, no. 2 (1981): 132–49.

4 National Research Council, *Education for Life and Work: Developing Transferable Knowledge and Skills in the 21st Century.* (Washington, DC: National Academies Press, 2012).

5 Peter A. Facione, *Critical Thinking: A Statement of Expert Consensus for Purposes of Educational Assessment and Instruction—The Delphi report,* (Millbrae, CA: The California Academic Press, 1990).

6 Göran Ingvar Broman and Karl-Henrik Robèrt, "A Framework for Strategic Sustainable Development," *Journal of Cleaner Production* 140 (2017): 17–31.

7 Junko Nakai, "Food and Agriculture Organization of the United Nations and the Sustainable Development Goals," *Sustainable Development* 22 (2018): 1–450.

8 Mark W. Rosegrant, Eduardo Magalhaes, Rowena A. Valmonte-Santos, and Daniel Mason-D'Croz, "Returns to Investment in Reducing Postharvest Food Losses and Increasing Agricultural Productivity Growth," *Prioritizing Development: A Cost Benefit Analysis of the United Nations' Sustainable Development Goals* (2018): 322–38; Jara Laso, Isabel García-Herrero, María Margallo, Lan Vázquez-Rowe, Pére Fullana, Alba Bala, Cristina Gazulla, Ángel Irabien, and Rubén Aldaco, "Finding an Economic and Environmental Balance in Value Chains Based on Circular Economy Thinking: An Eco-Efficiency Methodology Applied to the Fish Canning Industry," *Resources, Conservation and Recycling* 133 (2018): 428–37; Emiliano Lopez Barrera and Thomas Hertel, "Global Food Waste across the Income Spectrum: Implications for Food Prices, Production and Resource Use," *Food Policy* 98 (2021): 101874.

9 C. U. Ugonna, M. A. Jolaoso, and A. P. Onwualu, "Tomato Value Chain in Nigeria: Issues, Challenges and Strategies," *Journal of Scientific Research and Reports* 7, no. 7 (2015): 501–15.

10 Y. S. Cho, "인간과 디자인의 교감 빅터 파파넥" (Seoul, Republic of Korea: Designhouse, 2000).

11 Fabrizio Ceschin and Idil Gaziulusoy, "Evolution of Design for Sustainability: From Product Design to Design for System Innovations and Transitions," *Design Studies* 47 (2016): 118–63.

12 Cristina Sousa Rocha, Paula Antunes, and Paulo Partidário, "Design for Sustainability Models: A Multiperspective Review," *Journal of Cleaner Production* 234 (2019): 1428–45.

13 Sehun Oh, "From an Ecodesign Guide to a Sustainable Design Guide: Complementing Social Aspects of Sustainable Product Design Guidelines," *Archives of Design Research* 30, no. 2 (2017): 47–64.

14 Aguinaldo Dos Santos, Aline Krämer, and Carlo Vezzoli, "Design Brings Innovation to the Base of the Pyramid," *Design Management Review* 20, no. 2 (2009): 78–85.

15 Leonardo Gomez Castillo, Jan Carel Diehl, and J. C. Brezet, "Design Considerations for Base of the Pyramid (BoP) Projects," in *Proceedings of the Northern World Mandate: Cumulus Helsinki Conference*. (Helsinki, Finland: 2012). http://cumulushelsinki2012.aalto.fi/academic_papers/index.html.

16 Carla M. Evans, *Measuring Student Success Skills: A Review of the Literature on Collaboration*. (Dover, NH: National Center for the Improvement of Educational Assessment, 2020).

17 Carol E. Feingold, Martha D. Cobb, and Joanna Arnold, "Student Perceptions of Team Learning in Nursing Education," *Journal of Nursing Education* 47, no. 5 (2008): 214; Karen E. Pugsley and Laura H. Clayton, "Traditional Lecture or Experiential Learning: Changing Student Attitudes," *Journal of Nursing Education* 42, no. 11 (2003): 520–23; Patty Coker, "Effects of an Experiential Learning Program on the Clinical Reasoning and Critical Thinking Skills of Occupational Therapy Students," *Journal of Allied Health* 39, no. 4 (2010): 280–86.

18 Charles C. Bonwell and James A. Eison, *Active Learning: Creating Excitement in the Classroom*. 1991 ASHE-ERIC Higher Education Reports

(Washington, DC: Eric Clearinghouse on Higher Education, The George Washington University, 1991).

19 Steve Olusegun Bada and Steve Olusegun Bada, "Constructivism Learning Theory: A Paradigm for Teaching and Learning," *Journal of Research & Method in Education* 5, no. 6 (2015): 66–70.

20 Scott Freeman, Sarah L. Eddy, Miles McDonough, Michelle K. Smith, Nnadozie Okoroafor, Hannah Jordt, and Mary Pat Wenderoth, "Active Learning Increases Student Performance in Science, Engineering, and Mathematics," *Proceedings of the National Academy of Sciences* 111, no. 23 (2014): 8410–15.

21 Janet R. McColl-Kennedy, Anders Gustafsson, Elina Jaakkola, Phil Klaus, Zoe Jane Radnor, Helen Perks, and Margareta Friman, "Fresh Perspective on Customer Experience," *Journal of Services Marketing* 29, no. 6/7 (2015): 430–435; Llewellyn Mann, Rosemary Chang, Siva Chandrasekaran, Alicen Coddington, Scott Daniel, Emily Cook, Enda Crossin et al., "From Problem-Based Learning to Practice-Based Education: A Framework for Shaping Future Engineers," *European Journal of Engineering Education* 46, no. 1 (2021): 27–47.

22 Rebecca McLaughlan and Jason M. Lodge, "Facilitating Epistemic Fluency through Design Thinking: A Strategy for the Broader Application of Studio Pedagogy within Higher Education," *Teaching in Higher Education* 24, no. 1 (2019): 81–97.

23 Cecilie Anvik, Janikke Solstad Vedeler, Charlotte Wegener, Åshild Slettebø, and Atle Ødegård, "Practice-Based Learning and Innovation in Nursing Homes," *Journal of Workplace Learning* 32, no. 2 (2020): 122–34.

24 Hollis and Eren, "Implementation of Real-world Experiential Learning in a Food Science Course Using a Food Industry-integrated Approach," 109–19.

25 D. E. Matzembacher, R. L. Gonzales, and L. F. M. do Nascimento, "From Informing to Practicing: Students' Engagement Through Practice-Based Learning Methodology and Community Services," *The International Journal of Management Education* 17, no. 2(2019): 191–200.

26 Mann, Llewellyn, Rosemary Chang, Siva Chandrasekaran, Alicen Coddington, Scott Daniel, Emily Cook, Enda Crossin et al., "From Problem-based Learning to Practice-based Education: A Framework for Shaping Future Engineers," *European Journal of Engineering Education* 46, no. 1 (2021): 27–47.

27 Jan Herrington and Ron Oliver, "An Instructional Design Framework for Authentic Learning Environments," *Educational Technology Research and Development* (2000): 23–48.

28 Richard Buchanan, "Wicked Problems in Design Thinking," *Design Issues* 8, no. 2 (1992): 5–21.

29 Horst Rittel, "Wicked Problems," *Management Science* 4, no. 14 (December 1967).

30 Debra Rowe, "Education for a Sustainable Future," *Science* 317, no. 5836 (2007): 323, 324.

31 Han Brezet and Carolien van Hemel, *Ecodesign, A Promising Approach to Sustainable Production and Consumption.* (Paris, France: United Nations Environment Programme, Industry and Environment, Cleaner Production; The Hauge: Rathenau Institute; Delft, Netherlands: Delft University of Technology, 1997).

32 Kasee J. Hildenbrand and Judy A. Schultz, "Development of a Rubric to Improve Critical Thinking," *Athletic Training Education Journal* 7, no. 3 (2012): 86–94; William Condon and Diane Kelly-Riley, "Assessing and Teaching What We Value: The Relationship between College-Level Writing and Critical Thinking Abilities," *Assessing Writing* 9, no. 1 (2004): 56–75.
33 Andrew L. Oros, "Let's Debate: Active Learning Encourages Student Participation and Critical Thinking," *Journal of Political Science Education* 3, no. 3 (2007): 293–311; Julie Martyn, Ruth Terwijn, Megan Y. C. A. Kek, and Henk Huijser, "Exploring the Relationships between Teaching, Approaches to Learning and Critical Thinking in a Problem-based Learning Foundation Nursing Course," *Nurse Education Today* 34, no. 5 (2014): 829–35.
34 Ian J. Quitadamo and Martha J. Kurtz, "Learning to Improve: Using Writing to Increase Critical Thinking Performance in General Education Biology," *CBE – Life Sciences Education* 6, no. 2 (2007): 140–54.

Bibliography

Anvik, Cecilie, Janikke Solstad Vedeler, Charlotte Wegener, Åshild Slettebø, and Atle Ødegård. "Practice-based Learning and Innovation in Nursing Homes." *Journal of Workplace Learning* 32, no. 2 (2020): 122–34.
Bada, Steve Olusegun, and Steve Olusegun. "Constructivism Learning Theory: A Paradigm for Teaching and Learning." *Journal of Research & Method in Education* 5, no. 6 (2015): 66–70.
Barrera, Emiliano Lopez, and Thomas Hertel. "Global Food Waste across the Income Spectrum: Implications for Food Prices, Production and Resource Use." *Food Policy* 98 (2021): 101874.
Bonwell, Charles C., and James A. Eison. "Active Learning: Creating Excitement in the Classroom." 1991 ASHE-ERIC Higher Education Reports. Washington, DC: ERIC Clearinghouse on Higher Education, The George Washington University, 1991.
Brame, Cynthia J. "Active learning." *Vanderbilt University Center for Teaching, 2016.* https://cft.vanderbilt.edu/active-learning/ (Accessed May 31, 2024).
Brezet, Han and Carolien van Hemel, *Ecodesign, A Promising Approach to Sustainable Production and Consumption.* (Paris, France: United Nations Environment Programme, Industry and Environment, Cleaner Production; The Hauge: Rathenau Institute; Delft, Netherlands: Delft University of Technology, 1997).
Broman, Göran Ingvar, and Karl-Henrik Robèrt. "A Framework for Strategic Sustainable Development." *Journal of Cleaner Production* 140 (2017): 17–31.
Buchanan, Richard. "Wicked Problems in Design Thinking." *Design Issues* 8, no. 2 (1992): 5–21.
Castillo, Leonardo Gomez, Jan Carel Diehl, and J. C. Brezet. "Design Considerations for Base of the Pyramid (BoP) Projects. *Proceeding of the Northern World Mandate: Cumulus Helsinki Conference.* Helsinki, Finland. (2012). Retrieved from http://cumulushelsinki2012.aalto.fi/academic_papers/index.html.
Ceschin, Fabrizio, and Idil Gaziulusoy. "Evolution of Design for Sustainability: From Product Design to Design for System Innovations and Transitions." *Design Studies* 47 (2016): 118–63.

Coker, Patty. "Effects of an Experiential Learning Program on the Clinical Reasoning and Critical Thinking Skills of Occupational Therapy Students." *Journal of Allied Health* 39, no. 4 (2010): 280–86.

Condon, William, and Diane Kelly-Riley. "Assessing and Teaching What We Value: The Relationship between College-level Writing and Critical Thinking Abilities." *Assessing Writing* 9, no. 1 (2004): 56–75.

Cummins, Jim. "Age on Arrival and Immigrant Second Language Learning in Canada: A Reassessment1." *Applied linguistics* 2, no. 2 (1981): 132–49.

Dos Santos, Aguinaldo, Aline Krämer, and Carlo Vezzoli. "Design Brings Innovation to the Base of the Pyramid." *Design Management Review* 20, no. 2 (2009): 78–85.

Evans, Carla M. *Measuring Student Success Skills: A Review of the Literature on Collaboration.* Dover, NH: National Center for the Improvement of Educational Assessment, 2020.

Facione, Peter A. *Critical Thinking: A Statement of Expert Consensus for Purposes of Educational Assessment and Instruction—The Delphi Report.* Millbrae, CA: The California Academic Press, 1990.

Feingold, Carol E., Martha D. Cobb, and Joanna Arnold. "Student Perceptions of Team Learning in Nursing Education." *Journal of Nursing Education* 47, no. 5 (2008): 214.

Freeman, Scott, Sarah L. Eddy, Miles McDonough, Michelle K. Smith, Nnadozie Okoroafor, Hannah Jordt, and Mary Pat Wenderoth. "Active Learning Increases Student Performance in Science, Engineering, and Mathematics." *Proceedings of the National Academy of Sciences* 111, no. 23 (2014): 8410–15.

Herrington, Jan, and Ron Oliver. "An Instructional Design Framework for Authentic Learning Environments." *Educational Technology Research and Development* (2000): 23–48.

Hildenbrand, Kasee J., and Judy A. Schultz. "Development of a Rubric to Improve Critical Thinking." *Athletic Training Education Journal* 7, no. 3 (2012): 86–94.

Hollis, Francine H., and Fulya Eren. "Implementation of Real-world Experiential Learning in a Food Science Course Using a Food Industry-integrated Approach." *Journal of Food Science Education* 15, no. 4 (2016): 109–19.

Jarvis, Peter, ed. *The Theory and Practice of Teaching.* London: Routledge, 2006.

Laso, Jara, Isabel García-Herrero, María Margallo, Ian Vázquez-Rowe, Pére Fullana, Alba Bala, Cristina Gazulla, Ángel Irabien, and Rubén Aldaco. "Finding an Economic and Environmental Balance in Value Chains Based on Circular Economy Thinking: An Eco-Efficiency Methodology Applied to the Fish Canning Industry." *Resources, Conservation and Recycling* 133 (2018): 428–37.

Mann, Llewellyn, Rosemary Chang, Siva Chandrasekaran, Alicen Coddington, Scott Daniel, Emily Cook, Enda Crossin et al. "From Problem-based Learning to Practice-based Education: A Framework for Shaping Future Engineers." *European Journal of Engineering Education* 46, no. 1 (2021): 27–47.

Martyn, Julie, Ruth Terwijn, Megan Y. C. A. Kek, and Henk Huijser. "Exploring the Relationships between Teaching, Approaches to Learning and Critical Thinking in a Problem-based Learning Foundation Nursing Course." *Nurse Education Today* 34, no. 5 (2014): 829–35.

Matzembacher, D. E., R. L. Gonzales, and L. F. M. do Nascimento. "From Informing to Practicing: Students' Engagement through Practice-based Learning Methodology and Community Services." *The International Journal of Management Education* 17, no. 2 (2019): 191–200.

McColl-Kennedy, Janet R., Anders Gustafsson, Elina Jaakkola, Phil Klaus, Zoe Jane Radnor, Helen Perks, and Margareta Friman. "Fresh Perspective on Customer Experience." *Journal of Services Marketing* 29, no. 6/7 (2015): 430–435.

McLaughlan, Rebecca, and Jason M. Lodge. "Facilitating Epistemic Fluency Through Design Thinking: A Strategy for the Broader Application of Studio Pedagogy within Higher Education." *Teaching in Higher Education* 24, no. 1 (2019): 81–97.

Nakai, Junko. "Food and Agriculture Organization of the United Nations and the Sustainable Development Goals." *Sustainable Development* 22 (2018): 1–450.

National Research Council. *Education for Life and Work: Developing Transferable Knowledge and Skills in the 21st Century*. Washington, DC: National Academies Press, 2012.

Oh, Sehun. "From an Ecodesign Guide to a Sustainable Design Guide: Complementing Social Aspects of Sustainable Product Design Guidelines." *Archives of Design Research* 30, no. 2 (2017): 47–64.

Oros, Andrew L. "Let's Debate: Active Learning Encourages Student Participation and Critical Thinking." *Journal of Political Science Education* 3, no. 3 (2007): 293–311.

Pugsley, Karen E., and Laura H. Clayton. "Traditional Lecture or Experiential Learning: Changing Student Attitudes." *Journal of Nursing Education* 42, no. 11 (2003): 520–23.

Quitadamo, Ian J., and Martha J. Kurtz. "Learning to Improve: Using Writing to Increase Critical Thinking Performance in General Education Biology." *CBE – Life Sciences Education* 6, no. 2 (2007): 140–54.

Rittel, Horst. "Wicked Problems." *Management Science* 4, no. 14 (December 1967).

Rocha, Cristina Sousa, Paula Antunes, and Paulo Partidário. "Design for Sustainability Models: A Multiperspective Review." *Journal of Cleaner Production* 234 (2019): 1428–45.

Rosegrant, Mark W., Eduardo Magalhaes, Rowena A. Valmonte-Santos, and Daniel Mason-D'Croz. "Returns to Investment in Reducing Postharvest Food Losses and Increasing Agricultural Productivity Growth." *Prioritizing Development: A Cost Benefit Analysis of the United Nations' Sustainable Development Goals* (2018): 322–38.

Rowe, Debra. "Education for a Sustainable Future." *Science* 317, no. 5836 (2007): 323–24.

Scriven, Michael and Richard Paul. "Defining Critical Thinking," Statement by Micheal Scriven and Richard Paul in *8th Annual International Conference on Critical Thinking and Education Reform*, Summer 1987. http://www.criticalthinking.org/pages/defining-critical-thinking/766.

Ugonna, C. U., M. A. Jolaoso, and A. P. Onwualu. "Tomato Value Chain in Nigeria: Issues, Challenges and Strategies." *Journal of Scientific Research and Reports* 7, no. 7 (2015): 501–15.

Živković, Slaĺana. "A Model of Critical Thinking as an Important Attribute for Success in the 21st Century." *Procedia-social and Behavioral Sciences* 232 (2016): 102–8.

5 Aftercare

A Cross-Cultural Classroom to Practice Empathetic Design

Andrea Sosa Fontaine and Tina Patel

Introduction

People live, work, occupy, and identify with their built environments. These spaces are in constant flux, influenced by socio-political and ecological climates, structural and systemic injustice, prejudice and conflict in the world around us. With contemporary global concerns and demands for action in response to the historical marginalization of Black, Indigenous and People of Color (BIPOC populations), educators are facing complex decisions about how to respond through design curricula. While there has been a shift at the institutional level to support initiatives for diversity, equity and inclusion, there has been a mixed response at the program level.[1] Some design educators have diversified course content, introduced complex subjects and expanded studio pedagogy. An apparent solution in design education is the integration of community engagement projects in the design studios, either on a passive or active level.[2] We need to think beyond the obvious and consider what other teaching methods and approaches can be used to develop students into empathetic thinkers while tackling these complex issues.

This chapter focuses on a joint elective course, titled *Aftercare,* taught between two undergraduate interior design programs in the US and Lebanon as a case study highlighting one such unique approach. The course presented ideas of how designers build empathy and care for people and the built environment impacted by socio-political and ecological climates, turmoil and conflicts. Through exposure to diverse perspectives, difficult conversations and new connections with peers on the other side of the world, our students learned to practice design with empathy and care. We will highlight how this course evolved, its structure and organization and pedagogical approach, and will conclude with student and faculty reflections. Starting a dialogue about expanding pedagogical responses to current and ongoing global and local turmoil will hopefully lead to the repositioning of interior design education and effectively better prepare our students to be compassionate global citizens and community stewards.

DOI: 10.4324/9781032705927-6

Design Education as it Exists

An Analysis of Our Curriculum

From the climate crisis to wealth inequality, political inefficiencies, pandemics, and insufficient education and healthcare systems, global crises demand innovative and empathetic responses from designers. While activist movements have begun to address racism, economic injustice and climate change, design education must adapt to equip students with tools to respond to real-world disparities in our complex social and ecological landscape. Design pedagogy and pedagogues have an ethical responsibility to prepare students to address both ecological and social issues, such as inequality, human rights violations and the local and global community.[3] Education is a social process and should emphasize the exploration of issues-based curricula that deal with these local and global concerns.[4] As a foundation, we need to develop a theoretical framing for design education based on social issues, viewing it as a process of discovering solutions that are tailored to be in alignment with the needs of the surrounding context, rather than merely aiming for a quick fix. This approach demands a holistic understanding and profound social expertise within the context in which the proposed solutions will eventually operate.[5] As social and political landscapes transform, it becomes crucial to dismantle the systemic barriers that exist within design education so that students can understand their role as future designers, and subsequent social responsibility. This new knowledge should emerge through self and collective reflection, invention, and re-invention, a hopeful method of inquiry that human beings pursue in the world, with the world, and with each other.[6] This also requires shifting discourses from solely researching and defining the culture of communities to teaching our students about how culture is both constructed and produced.[7] Within this context, we should address issues of colonization, globalization, immigration and power differentials. At the core of these models, it is essential to foster cultural and multicultural understanding in design education to enhance our students' capacity for empathetic thinking.[8]

These provocations provided us the momentum to critically assess our current interior design curriculum,[9] which is based on a framework with multiple levels of technical and representation courses that are linked to support design studios. History/theory and research courses are introduced later, after foundational design skills are developed to foster critical, discursive and creative thinking. This pragmatic approach effectively develops skills and meets the requirements of the accreditation standards for a professional degree.[10] Teaching the intricacies of cultural sensitivity is a challenging and lengthy endeavor. The very nature of culture, with its inherent complexity, presents an intellectual and ethical hurdle for aspiring designers. Often, cultural education takes place within a studio setting, which serves as the primary platform for students to acquire essential design skills. However, limited interactions and readings within the studio environment can lead to oversimplified generalizations that fail to capture the identities and rich nuances inherent in different cultures.

This curriculum development prompted the following questions:

1. What teaching methods and approaches exist to educate our students on complex local and global issues?
2. Are we providing opportunities for students to practice in a global society, understanding how to work with cultures and communities beyond their own?
3. What role does empathy play in design practice and education?
4. Finally, are we continuing to identify biases that exist in ourselves as educators, within our students and the structures of our curriculum?

While our curriculum offers an opportunity for students to connect with other communities through some studio projects, there are currently no core curriculum courses that holistically address how people and the built environment are impacted by socio-political and ecological conflicts on a global scale. This led us to develop an elective course called "Aftercare", in partnership with the Lebanese American University (LAU) to create a cross-cultural classroom experience for both students and design educators. We believe that crafting a course of this nature creates a supportive community among like-minded educators who share similar values. Additionally, with peers from different nationalities, who are learning interior design on another continent, the course establishes a strong foundation for students to engage in meaningful cultural explorations and learning experiences throughout the semester.

Interior Design as it Exists

An Analysis of Our Learners and Educators

While the course was developed as a response to the many local and global socio-political and ecological issues that continue to impact the built environment, as a critical point of context, we will offer a reflection on the cultural diversity of our own students, faculty and the professional practice of interior design. We must also acknowledge that the cultural identity of our students, faculty and practice is not reflective of the often BIPOC communities that are most greatly impacted by these issues.

Interior Design began as a professional practice for women, outside of architecture, with a focus on domestic interior decoration. However, the discipline has since expanded to include commercial interior design practices that require a formal postsecondary education, and a professional qualification examination. While our discipline has shifted from its origins, we continue to see that there has been slower progress in expanding the cultural diversity of those who practice interior design, particularly within North America.[11]More specifically, those who are practicing interior design often become a reflection of those who have access to a postsecondary interior design education. If we want to see more diverse practitioners in the profession, then we need to expand the diversity of those who can access interior design education by identifying and removing systemic barriers.

Prior to the COVID-19 pandemic, our interior design student body was slightly more diverse than it is today; however, this was primarily due to the presence of a small number of international students, which dwindled following border restrictions during the height of the pandemic. In fact, our student body has always lacked diversity and is not representative of the region where our campus is situated. Our campus is in a college town, where most of our students either relocate or commute to,[12] for their design education. With the largest surrounding counties, there is significant racial diversity, with more than 40% of the population not identifying as white.[13] However, in comparison to the composition of our interior design student body based on the most recent statistical data from 2021,[14] we can see that our students overwhelmingly do not reflect the regional diversity where our campus is located.[15] Furthermore, there exists a similar disparity in the diversity of the faculty within our college. As such, we must recognize this as a contributing factor to the context of our course. While the intention of a cross-cultural course is to provide direct opportunities for cross-cultural connections between students, we must acknowledge the additional work that needs to be done at the level of interior design education to expand the diversity of our student body to accurately reflect our surrounding communities, and to also provide cross-cultural interactions among their own local cohort of peers.

Paradoxical View on Care and Aftercare: Why "Aftercare"?

"*Aftercare*" is both a recognition and an action. It begins with the recognition of the long-term implications of the influences and events on people, spaces and communities, followed by the action of care by way of an empathetic response. Whether these implications emerge over time or are a result of an acute event, care or aftercare becomes an exercise of weaving together threads, mending gaps and amplifying muted voices.[16] Is it possible to use care as a design strategy to create environments that promulgate long-term and equitable experiences rather than a remedial measure? Care is often overlooked in the production of the built environment. In architecture, care is predominantly demonstrated through maintenance and the findings of post-occupancy evaluations, which assess how a building is inhabited compared to how it was intended to be used during design. It is commonly viewed as a tool for measuring performance, an evaluation of the level of care needed after construction which is one way to measure the success of the building. Interior space is where people spend most of their time and experience their lives, and therefore, interior design is a practice that responds to the circumstances of peoples' lives, and often begins with understanding the circumstances of individual people and their communities.

If we utilize care as a framework for analysis, imagination and response, design practitioners and legislators in conjunction with community members might have the momentum needed to establish more equitable and responsible futures.[17] Caring for the interior or built environment involves recognizing its significance as both a contributor to, and record keeper of, both collective and individual quality of life. Consequently, care can serve to convey the stories of a building's history and act as a conduit for its future potential. Jorge Otero-Pailos, a historic preservation artist, employs the practice of care in various environments, not only to restore their condition but also to extract narratives from them. Care is an attitude that necessitates a mindset emphasizing intricate human connections and their preservation through the thoughtful application of considerations to the environments that are both cared for and subsequently occupied.[18]

In response to the global issues that we are living in and the state of design education, we started discussions about the role of designers in the world and our role as educators. At the same time, we recognize the ways in which the built environment has harmed people and communities, and by extension, the contribution of designers and educators to this harm. We aim to facilitate reconciliation through the participatory design practices of care in the aftermath of harm, where care becomes both a feeling and response that extends empathy towards what already exists, while also supporting people and space beyond the construction of the built environment. This prompted us to define the primary goal of the elective as to expand practices of working with and understanding people, communities and places that are affected by historical and current structural inequities, systemic injustices, ecological impacts and socio-political conflicts, resulting in new cross-cultural pedagogical models of care and aftercare.

Aftercare: Organization and Structure of the Course

The elective course, Aftercare, was developed in partnership with Lebanese American University (LAU) and Kent State University (KSU), and paired 15 undergraduate interior design students from each institution for a semester-long course. This partnership was formed as an extension of previous collaborations between our two institutions. The primary learning objective of this course was to develop an understanding of how socio-political and ecological climates, turmoil and conflict can have a significant impact on people and places. We asked ourselves, *What are the long-term consequences of these events on spaces and communities, and were they developed over time or as a result of an acute response?* The primary provocation of the course was explored under the following topics represented in Figure 5.1:

Empathy: the students were introduced to the modes and methods to design with empathy for people in different physical, social and cultural contexts.

After Disaster: discussed power inequalities, political unrest, cultural conflict and gender-based discrimination and how we can design spaces where individuals, families and entire cultures can inhabit without fear or discrimination.

Care for Built Environment: focused on issues of social and environmental justice, ecological impact, heritage and memories.

Future of Care: identified both the opportunities and challenges that lie ahead of us, helping our students define their role as future practitioners.

We met remotely once a week to cover these five topics for 3 hours. Each of the topics was addressed in a three-part structure: faculty presentations on the topic for the first 45 minutes, followed by an external dialogue with invited guest speakers. Speakers varied and included urban designers, architects, activists and non-profits across the globe. They brought unique and diverse perspectives, often presenting harsh realities to our students prompting discussion about difficult issues as indicated in Figure 5.2. Each topic had a collection of assigned readings curated by the faculty, the last portion of each class focused on student group presentations and class discussions on readings where students shared unique perspectives and lived experiences. Further, students completed reflection assignments on the topical readings and conversation, which included the mechanisms of critical response, interviews, case study analysis, personal reflection and the development of a position statement on the issue. This allowed them to express their thoughts using writing and discussion on these critical issues through the lens of interior design theory and practice.

Aftercare: Pedagogy and Assignments

We realized that we needed to develop a theoretical framework for social design pedagogy as a process for discovering solutions where the designer aims to comprehend the environment rather than merely look for a solution.[19] As such, our pedagogical approach was to explore the topics reinforcing the core values of our discipline and those that exist at the periphery of the discipline. We designed assignments to broaden awareness and develop a deep social competency in both local and global issues.

ECONOMIC DIVIDE
POLITICAL UNREST
CULTURAL CONFLICT
GENDER BASED DISCRIMINATION

ENVIRONMENTAL JUSTICE
SOCIAL JUSTICE
SUSTAINABLE FOOTPRINT
HERITAGE AND MEMORIES

JUSTICE & INJUSTICE
MARGINALIZATION
INEQUALITY & DISPARITY
OPPORTUNITIES & CHALLENGES

GLOBAL AWARENESS
EMPATHY BUILDING
DEMOCRATIC THINKING

EMPATHY
AFTER DISASTER
CARE FOR BUILT ENVIRONMENT
CARE FOR PEOPLE
FUTURE OF CARE

AFTERCARE

Figure 5.1 Course content diagram

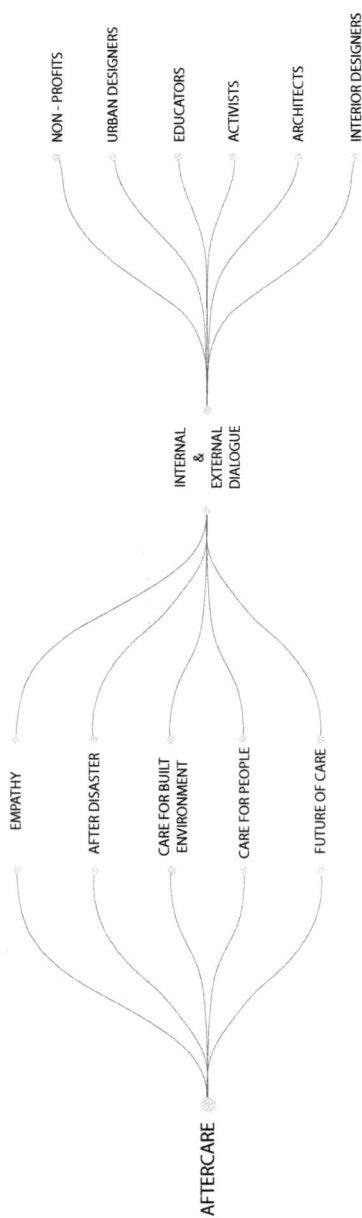

Figure 5.2 Course dialogue diagram

Care Package

We know that empathy would be a critical factor in both the structure and content of the course. Empathy is defined as the ability to identify, understand and feel other individuals' thoughts, feelings and circumstances, and respond consequently to them.[20] Empathetically designed spaces could improve and enrich people's physical, emotional and social interactions, adding value to the design responses.[21] Before learning to apply practices of empathy in interior design practice, we felt that it would be beneficial for students to engage with empathetic practices through their individual lived experiences. It was important to ask students to face their own biases about their new classmates from the other side of the world, as they would be approaching conversations of difficult subject matters throughout the semester. As such, we began the first class with a few exercises to build empathy, care and understanding among our KSU and LAU students. For the first assignment, called *The Digital Care Package*, each student was paired with a peer from the other university. The partners met with each other in a digital breakout room during the class and were given a series of prompts to get to know each other. The questions focused on hobbies, family life, favorite foods, motivation to become a designer, and hopes and dreams for the future. Often when students are paired into groups within a classroom, they dive right into an assignment before getting to know one another. As such, through the formality of the exercise, we presented an intentional opportunity for students to show understanding, while learning about their peer's identity through active listening and an extended conversation with identified deliverables. In addition, each student could decide what they wanted to share about their own culture, personality and experience as an interior design undergraduate student. Although students within the same interior design program may share similar experiences, there are often limited opportunities in a typical postsecondary classroom for students to speak about their own cultural identity The exercise gave students the space to share their experiences with someone who might be less familiar with the context but could understand through being in a similar program. After their discussions, each student was tasked to prepare a digital care package for their new peer. Inspired by both the care packages sent to students by their families during their first days of college, and the care packages that are provided in humanitarian circumstances, students considered how objects of familiarity and basic necessities could offer more than face value. As the students were peers in a remote classroom setting, and to avoid complications with costs to purchase and ship physical care packages, students were asked to create digital versions of their care packages for each other. Students were given examples of physical care packages, such as chicken soup left on one's doorstep or a t-shirt and toiletries that an airline might offer a stranded traveler. They were asked to consider how they could extend this same sentiment through digital care. Prior to beginning the exercise, the instructors allocated what they felt to be ample time for students to have a conversation using the prompts; however, when the

5-minute warning was given to prompt a return to the main classroom, many students asked for more time, as they were thoroughly engaged and enjoying the process of getting to know a new interior design peer.

Within their care packages, some students shared links to favorite objects, such as a sketchbook, pen or yoga mat, while not solely digital, provided a connection to their peers, while other students shared a favorite recipe, link to their digital playlist or even just a photograph of a favorite vacation spot. While the intention of the exercise was to ask students to engage in active listening and build trust as an introduction to empathy in design practice, the creation and receipt of the digital care packages led to unexpected outcomes. This discovery of shared interests led to the development of an immediate bond with their new classmate. The exercise was an acknowledgment that students had similar motivations for studying design, even though each student had a unique set of lived experiences. Many students also realized that they shared the same interests as their peers, including liking the same music, movies or even late-night snacks. While each student approached the exercise with some level of bias about their peers, they ended the exercise understanding that they lived very different lives within the context of being an undergraduate interior design student. In some cases, they had the same motivation for studying design, and some shared the same struggles and future career goals. Figure 5.3 shows examples of digital care packages that the students created for each other.

The second assignment extended the digital care package by asking students to apply the process to the context and scale of interior design practice. The students were introduced to the importance of building trust with communities where designers work in the same way that we asked them to build trust with their peers. In this practice, the interior designer is decentered, with community members and designers as equal participants in the process. Without knowing the specific community groups that students might work with in practice. The exercise tasked students with designing a card deck to help prompt conversations when working with new communities.[22] The cards offered an opportunity for students to consider the challenges faced in building new relationships and trust, as well as extracting pertinent information as a design facilitator. Students were asked to predict how they might understand both individuals and communities better when working in practice and to consider the challenges that they might face in gaining this understanding. Through the physical and familiar form of the card deck, students' design solutions were able to build trust when meeting communities for the first time through gamifying conversation starters for deeply complex and personal issues. Figure 5.4 shows some examples of this exercise.

Reflection Assignment

Reflection is a dialectical process that involves the interaction of multiple perspectives to develop an understanding of the content.[23] When we reflect,

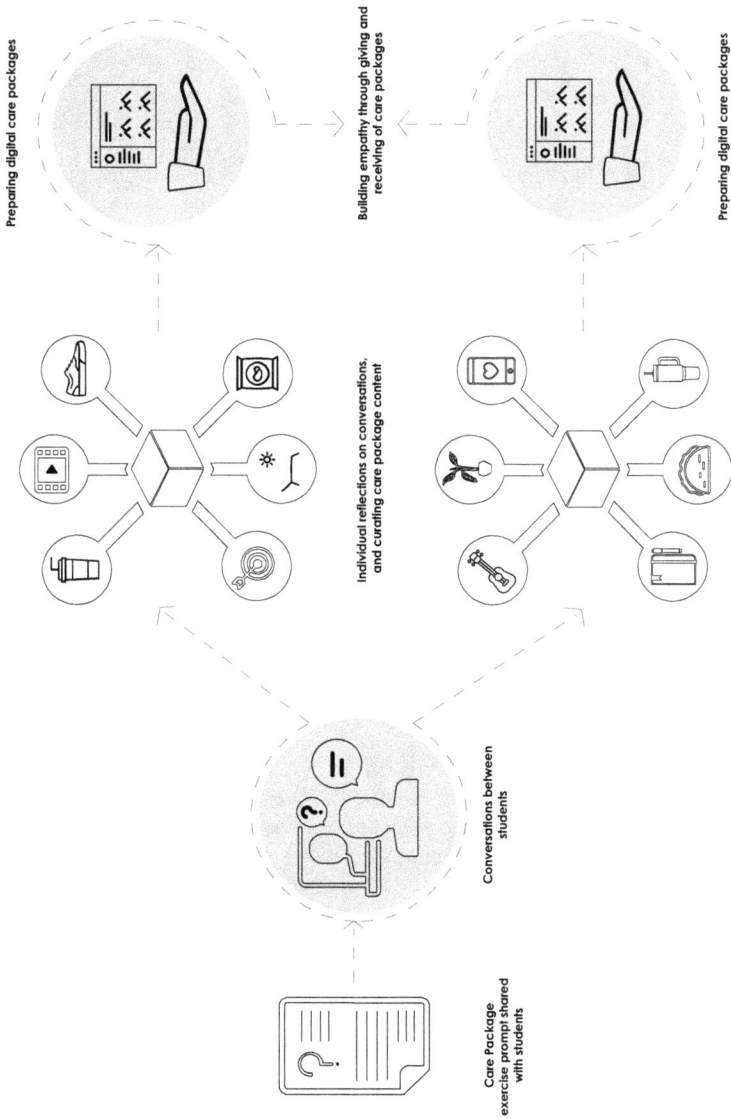

Figure 5.3 shows a diagram of the digital care package process.

Figure 5.4 Examples of the community card deck, developed by the student teams. Screenshot by the authors from the course digital whiteboard

we project and review, working pragmatically to find what we know, have learned and might understand. Reflective activities increase students' awareness of their thoughts and actions and their perceived recollection of experiences.[24] Instructors can facilitate various reflective activities, both guided and unguided (e.g., class discussion, journals, interviews, questioning, etc.). Following the care package and community card desk, the first two-week assignment focused on writing a reflection essay that included both a personal reflection and a critical response to the topical readings and discussions on economic divides, political unrest, cultural conflict and gender-based categorizations within the built environment. Student responses could be in agreement or disagreement, or an extension of the assigned readings. Students were asked, *How can we design interior spaces and places where individuals, families and entire cultures can inhabit without fear or discrimination?* This further led to the development of a position statement on the issue. The students considered how they see the article's main idea in the real world, how it influences them or others, and what are the causes, effects and potential solutions. They could agree, disagree, expand on the author's point or even extend the author's point in a different direction. They could respond by asking questions or questioning the author's main idea. They used the essay to critically examine their own beliefs and ideas on complex issues. They were asked to support their statements within the essay by citing the readings and by using one case study/precedent/project proposal from practice (design completed after 2000).

Reflection is not just an individual activity. Collaborative reflection might provide alternative insights when we engage with others; they perceive things differently or could challenge our preconceptions.[25] Within the context of this course, reflection assignments also provided an opportunity for students to take time outside of the discussions and reframe their thoughts, many of which changed after interactions with peers from the other institution. In addition, the reflection assignments reinforced the successful outcomes of the course content and speakers, as many of our students were progressively questioning the current and future role of interior design in a global context. For the second assignment, students worked in teams of two, identifying, documenting, analyzing and synthesizing an adaptive reuse project as a case study in a diverse community. Case studies represent real-world design projects, providing an opportunity to synthesize multiple pieces of information and demonstrate students' ability to make evaluative judgments. The students worked in teams of two to identify a recent project as the case study. The selected case study provided an orientation to the sensitivity and complexity of the practice of adaptability and reuse by recording the interrelationships of the existing built environment, its structure, materiality, context, memories and time. These recurring reflection activities encouraged students to make sense of the content, reimagine their experiences for future benefit and think critically about their thinking and writing practices. Their task involved a comprehensive documentation of this selected case study, encompassing not only textual descriptions but also visual elements such as images and annotated drawings. Furthermore, they were encouraged to engage with the original designer of the project, seeking insights to address a series of thought-provoking questions. These questions delved into the rationale behind preserving the space, the incorporation of obsolescence considerations, the pursuit of timelessness in design, the significance of authenticity in both design practices and the physical environment and the innovative dismantling techniques employed without compromising the sanctity of the space. Additionally, the students were prompted to analyze how various design elements, including surfaces, walls, floors and ceilings, were thoughtfully crafted to accommodate both short-term and long-term utility. This multifaceted endeavor culminated in a reflection report, which not only presented the documented findings but also synthesized the learning outcomes derived from the in-depth exploration of their chosen case study.

The reflective techniques, as diagramed in Figure 5.5, helped students become "producers" of knowledge rather than "consumers". Reflection, while it involves looking back, also serves as a mental rehearsal for future practice.[26]

Design Charrette

Phase II of this course focused on an immersive travel study to New York City (NYC). The initial intent was for both KSU and LAU students to travel together; however, due to pandemic constraints, LAU students traveled within

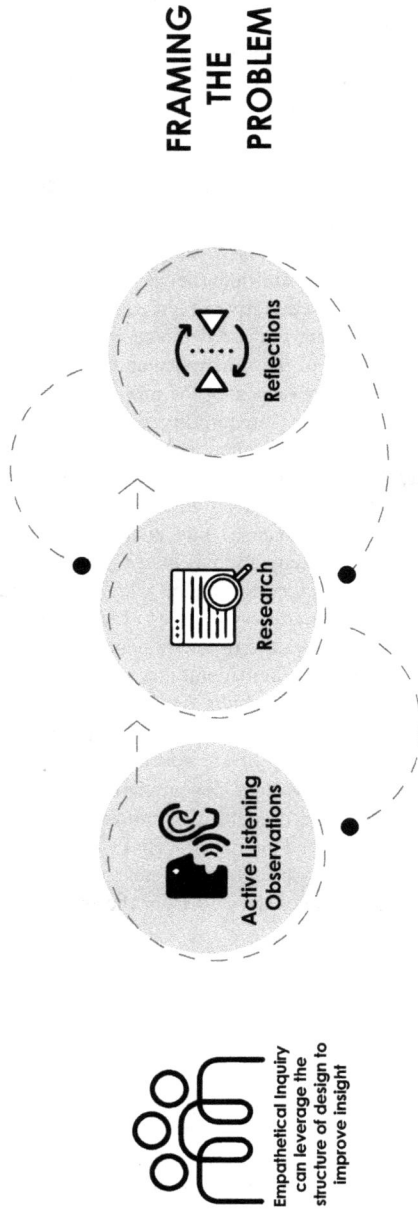

Figure 5.5 Reflective activity and empathy building

Beirut to an Armenian community called Bourj Hammoud. The purpose of the travel study was to support a design charrette, where students could apply the course content and learn to understand another community through empathetic design practice. As the course was intended for all students to travel to NYC, the content of this case study will focus on the KSU charrette which was situated in the Manhattan Chinatown of NYC. The travel study and charrette were developed as a response to the increase in xenophobia within the US, perpetuated by the COVID-19 pandemic. During the travel study, students were able to visit the community, explore and analyze the existing built environment through ethnographic studies, cultural workshops and guest speakers. In this charrette, students conducted participatory and immersive research to initiate design work within microneighborhoods. By observing community members, exploring the urban environment and immersing themselves in local customs, social habits, cuisine and craftsmanship, they practiced empathetic participatory design to create solutions that responded to community needs and identity. Our students had the opportunity to participate in a workshop with a Chinese cultural educator who spoke to our students about intercultural communication, including speech, mannerisms, dance and craft. Our students learned how to understand the cultural values of another community through the arts, food and historical context. Students were asked to develop a preliminary design proposal for a participatory space that fosters cross-cultural understanding and dialogue. The space needed to demonstrate a critical understanding of the community's existing cultural identity, including what has been sustained and lost over time, while simultaneously identifying and subsequently contributing to the dismantling of policies and structures that have marginalized them. The charrette provided an opportunity for students to reflect on the subjects and dialogue introduced in the first half of the course, and to demonstrate their understanding through an active design response.

As students prepared their responses to the prompt, they were given the flexibility to choose between an indoor or outdoor space, with an emphasis on creating an environment that paralleled the atmospheric characteristics of interior space, even if they chose an outdoor site. The students approached their proposals with intentionality, ensuring that their spatial concepts were crafted to avoid contributing to gentrification or perpetuating stereotypes. In their design responses, the students embraced a speculative approach, presenting their ideas through graphics and collages. While they did not fully detail or design the interior environment, their presentations included sufficient information to effectively communicate the intent behind their designs. Furthermore, students were encouraged to pair participation with a cultural value as part of the space program. They explored various combinations such as Retail + Participation, Food + Participation, Craft + Participation, and Exhibit + Participation, with the aim of integrating these elements into their design concepts.

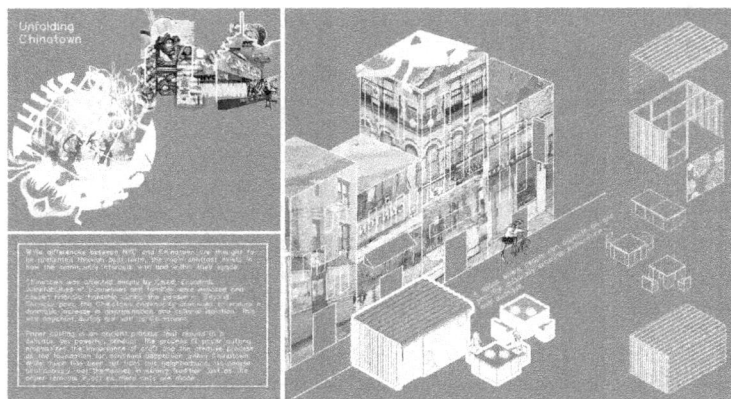

Figure 5.6 One example of a KSU student team design response. Digital poster created by Laina Brozost and Allison Baker, *Unfolding Chinatown,* April 2022, in the authors' possession.

Working with different communities with the same goal, the KSU and LAU students shared their work on a digital platform so that the dialogue that started at the beginning of the course could be continued about the charrette outcomes. Students understood the resilience and adaptability that the people of both communities had, in the way that they adapted their neighborhood to survive challenging times. Our students imagined a space where people can be educated on culturally sensitive topics, but also celebrate the beauty of the Chinese community in NYC. Figure 5.6 shows one of the student team projects, proposing a public space installation for the community to have meals and communal activities that were influenced by the ethos of Chinese paper cutting. Figure 5.7 represents the work of another group that observed public art and graffiti as moments of self-expression and restoration as they strolled through the streets in Chinatown, NYC. They crafted a place for artistic expression to communicate awareness and dialogue around the social injustices in this community.

Reflections

(Student reflection and instructors' retrospection to create a cross-cultural learning platform):

> Reflections throughout the course occurred both formally and informally. Through conversations with the instructors, responses to experiences, and course assignments we were able to gauge the immediate impact of this course on these students. During the trip to New York, we were able

BLENDING BOUNDARIES: CHINATOWN

Zach Skala, Faith DiLillo, & Olivia Wimberly - Aftercare: ID 30391 - Interior Design - CAED - Kent State University

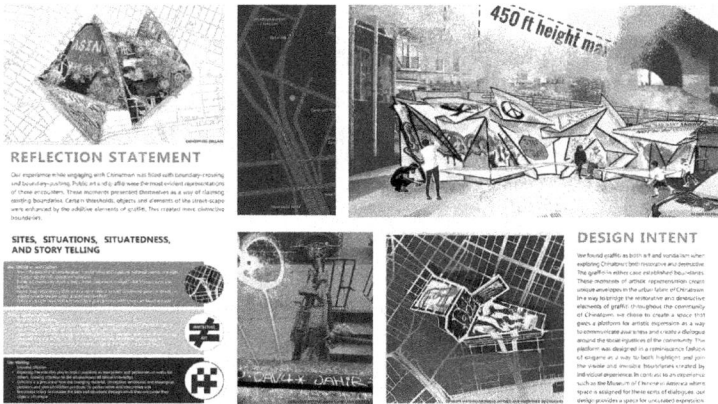

Figure 5.7 One example of KSU student team design response. Digital poster created by Zach Skala, Olivia Wimberly, and Faith DiLillo, *Blending Boundaries: Chinatown*, April 2022, in the authors' possession.

to spend extended time with our students beyond the typical classroom setting, including the sharing of meals, collective experiences at museums and navigating unfamiliar neighborhoods. For example, while visiting Chinatown in New York, we stopped with our students for lunch and learned that, for several of them, it was their first experience tasting dumplings or food flavored with Asian spices. While a surprise to the instructors, it reminded us that many of our students were still very young, some still living with their parents and some who have had limited experiences to engage with communities outside of their own. This experience was critical in expanding their understanding of the diversity in the world and their future role as interior designers.

At the end of the course, we asked our students to submit video reflections about their experience, thoughts on care and aftercare and their future roles in practice. Upon reflection of their overall experience students rated the following highly:

- Comprehension of many ideas and cultures
- Awareness of diversity
- Independence/interdependence
- Resilience
- Tolerance of ambiguity

Here are just a few quotes from those video submissions on care and aftercare and the impact of this course on their future practice:

> Care comes in many forms and begins with a way of thinking, not just an act.

> This course has taught me to consider and understand that everyone has different experiences. Some people have shared experiences, but they won't be the same. [We need to] take the time to listen and learn and be a student first to be respectful and empathetic.

> The course made me a better designer and a better person. The topics we touched on were tough to talk about but were enlightening . . . made us empathize.

Reflecting on the course content, we instructors believe that this experience increased students' sensitivity and understanding and made them empathetic towards each other, circumstances and impacts of social and ecological turmoil on people and the built environment. While the course content introduced students to expanded practices of care, it began through the simple interaction between students from KSU and LAU. This newly formed peer cohort allowed students to quickly find parallels in their life experiences as interior design students, but at the same time recognize and appreciate their differences. Through these simple peer interactions, they started to develop skills of cross-cultural communication, which will translate to their future roles in practice as interior designers. As an extension of this, during the travel study students posed questions of inquiry in response to the design charrette that reflected a sensitivity when working with other cultures and unfamiliar communities. Student reflections also demonstrated that they understand that skills of empathy and cross-cultural communication will be critical to their future practice as interior designers in an increasingly culturally diverse world. While the formal outcomes of the course exceeded expectations, the unexpected outcomes that we encountered and experienced during travel in a way became more significant. This helped us understand our student body, their lived experiences and exposure and understanding of cultural diversity better.

We also reflected on the assignments and exercises in the course and noted that the care package, which was the first exercise on the very first day of class, has potential outside of the context of this course. Although developed specifically for these students, the exercise could be implemented in any postsecondary interior design course to develop empathy and build a strong sense of community among peers. For example, a technical course might begin to introduce practices of care and cross-cultural understanding, even within very prescriptive learning outcomes. Introducing a care package exercise could provide an opportunity for a student to share their own cultural identity, subsequently fostering stronger peer relationships and a sense of belonging among students. Knowing and being exposed to diverse perspectives can contribute significantly to fostering more empathetic citizens. Furthermore, a care package could be equally adapted to be utilized by faculty to strengthen interdisciplinary partnerships and used in practice when working with new communities to build trust and make connections despite each person's unique identity and lived experiences.

We recognize that not all interior design courses have an obvious correlation with issues of social justice, but there are opportunities to implement practices of care in any course. For example, educators should begin any course with a review of the language of their syllabus, evaluating any language that might be limiting and ensuring that their required course textbooks and readings represent diverse global perspectives. Within the development of this elective course and in collaboration with our faculty peers from LAU, we selected course content, text and speakers representing diverse voices. As educators, we are acutely aware that publications validate content, but we also need to recognize that not all voices will be available through traditionally disseminated media. New media, such as podcasts and self-published narratives, could offer expanded diverse perspectives. It could require more effort from educators to find these resources but will offer a more diverse representation within course material.

This elective represents only the initial step in our reflective practice of interior design curricula, prompting us to delve into several important questions. Firstly, we contemplated how this course has reignited our motivation for reimagining pedagogical approaches, research methodologies and practical applications within our discipline with a central focus on care as a guiding principle. We also reflected on ways in which we can embed the concept of care into our design thinking, making it a fundamental aspect of how we approach the creation of spaces and products for both people and places. We stay committed to exploring uncharted territories in the realm of design education, seeking innovative ways to foster a more profound connection between design and diverse cultural contexts. These questions of reflection are in alignment with our ongoing commitment to enhance and evolve the field of interior design, decenter the interior designer, inspire new perspectives and promote a more inclusive and empathetic approach within our community.

Future Directives

The primary goal of this course was to develop a cross-cultural pedagogical model of care and aftercare to deepen our understanding of the people and places affected by historical and current structural inequities, systemic injustices and socio-political and ecological conflicts on both a local and global scale. Our partnership with interior design faculty, students and guest speakers across the globe helped us achieve that goal. It encouraged us to take advantage of the ongoing global and local turmoil to reposition design education to advance our discipline and prepare our students to be global citizens, democratic thinkers and community stewards.

As educators, we need to not only reflect on the diversity of the students who enroll in our courses but also acknowledge the reasons that might prevent some students from accessing interior design education. We are certain that there are systemic issues where perhaps cost and the geographic location of our campus might be a hindrance to increasing the diversity of our student cohorts. A commitment to challenging these barriers to access interior design education is necessary among the profession of interior design, faculty and institutions. Even those of us who are already doing work in this area, like ourselves, know that we need to reflect on our own privileges and biases. In the meantime, we must continue to ask our students to reflect on their own lived experiences and identities as they approach their work as future designers, learning to decenter themselves and establish design practices to work with communities. This course has encouraged us to network and build connections with institutions and experts across the globe to expose our students to a diverse perspective on issues. Through this network, we have come to realize that our concerns are not specific to our region but are common throughout much of North America, and in different capacities among our global peers. We are hopeful for the future in that we have come to realize that these issues are increasingly a priority for students, design educators and practitioners, and many others are supportive of this need for more work to be done.

While this elective is just the beginning, educators collectively can further establish best practices that can be incorporated into studios, seminars and/or other courses. It will advance our discipline but will be an evolutionary process of discovery, connection, reflection, contribution and impact. To truly evaluate the impact of this course on future interior designers, perhaps a survey of students a few years after entering practice could offer some validation. However, regardless of what students remember from the specific course content, they have learned to become more empathetic design thinkers through their experiences in the course, and they can go on to seek cross-cultural connections through the collective human experience as opposed to looking for what divides us. Here we can also recognize that only a small fraction of our students were able to enroll in the elective course and participate in these complex discussions and experiences. While our curriculum offers space for one studio project to be dedicated to issues of social justice, this is simply not enough and may be perceived outwardly as a performative act. In such cases, we can still create meaningful experiences for all our students. In developing studio projects, we can find synergetic collaborations that will help us create meaningful experiences for both our students and the communities that we work with. If only more people followed these practices, we would likely see spaces being designed and utilized with a bit more care.

Notes

1 Carl Matthews, Ngozi Brown, and Michaela Brooks, "Confronting Lack of Student Diversity in Interior Design Education," *Journal of Interior Design* 46, no. 4 (2021): 3–11, https://doi.org/10.1111/joid.12207.
2 Tasoulla Hadjiyanni, "Decolonizing Interior Design Education," *Journal of Interior Design* 45, no. 2 (2020): 3–9, https://doi.org/10.1111/joid.12170.
3 Carolina Gill, Peter Chan, and Peter Kwok, "Re-envisioning a Design Curriculum," Paper presented at *DesignEd Asia Conference, Convention and Exhibition Centre,* Hong Kong, 2010, http://dx.doi.org/10.13140/2.1.4438.1449
4 John Dewey, *Experience and Education* (New York: Free Press, 2015).
5 Neeta Verma, "Developing a Pedagogy for Social Design," Paper presented at *The SEGD Academic Summit,* Miami, FL, June 2017.
6 Paulo Freire and Myra Ramos Bergman, *Pedagogy of the Oppressed: 50th-anniversary Edition* (New York: Bloomsbury Academic, 2018).
7 Renato I. Rosaldo, *Culture and Truth: Remaking of Social Analysis* (Boston: Beacon Press, 1993).
8 Tasoulla Hadjiyanni, "Rethinking Culture in Interior Design Pedagogy: The Potential beyond CIDA Standard 2G," *Journal of Interior Design* 38, no. 3 (2013): 5–12, https://doi.org/10.1111/joid.12013.
9 The authors of this paper worked in conjunction with the Kent State University Interior Design Program Committee and were part of developing the curriculum that is being evaluated in this paper.
10 Within the state of Ohio, a Professional Interior Design degree is one that meets CIDA (Council for Interior Design Accreditation) standards.
11 Christine M. Piotrowski, *Professional Practice for Interior Designers* (Hoboken, NJ: John Wiley and Sons, Inc., 2020).
12 Kent State University. Center for Student Involvement, Resources, 2023, accessed September 13, 2023, https://www.kent.edu/node/60841.
13 Ian Cross, "2020 Census: Cleveland, Cuyahoga County Lose Thousands of Residents; Northeast Ohio More Diverse," *News 5 Cleveland WEWS,* August 13, 2021, https://www.news5cleveland.com/news/local-news/2020-census-cleveland-cuyahoga-county-lose-thousands-of-residents-northeast-ohio-more-diverse.
14 Ibid.
15 Media Factual, "The Interior Design Major at Kent State University at Kent," *College Factual,* accessed September 12, 2023, https://www.collegefactual.com/colleges/kent-state-university-at-kent/academic-life/academic-majors/visual-and-performing-arts/design-and-applied-arts/interior-design/#:~:text=Kent%20State%20Interior%20Design%20Bachelor%27s,men%20and%2097%25%20were%20women.
16 Shannon Mattern, "Maintenance and Care," *Places Journal,* no. 2018 (2018), https://doi.org/10.22269/181120.
17 Graeme Brooker, "Inner-Propriations: Degrowing the Interior," in *Appropriated Interiors,* ed. Deborah Schneiderman, Anca I. Lasc, and Karin Tehve (New York: Routledge, 2022), 183–204.
18 Jorge Otero-Pailos, "Monumentaries," in *Tabula Plena: Forms of Urban Preservation,* ed. Byrony Roberts (Zurich: Lars Muller, 2016).

19 Ibid.
20 David Howe, *Empathy: What It Is and Why It Matters* (Houndmills, Basingstoke, Hampshire: Palgrave Macmillan, 2013).
21 Fabio Tellez-Bohorquez, "Empathy Expression and Development in Industrial Design Education," in *9th International Conference on Design and Emotion 2014: The Colors of Care* (Universidad de los Andes, Columbia, 2014), 256–59.
22 This exercise was in part inspired by the "Peace and Justice" cards developed by *Designing Justice + Designing Spaces,* https://designingjustice.org/peace-and-justice-cards/.
23 Kathleen Blake Yancey, *Reflection in the Writing Classroom* (Boulder, CO: NetLibrary, Inc., 1999).
24 Douglas P. Larsen, Daniel A. London, and Amanda R. Emke, "Using Reflection to Influence Practice: Student Perceptions of Daily Reflection in Clinical Education," *Perspectives on Medical Education* 5, no. 5 (2016): 285–91, https://doi.org/10.1007/s40037-016-0293-1.
25 Daniel G. Krutka, Daniel J. Bergman, Raymond Flores, Katherine Mason, and Ashlie R. Jack, "Microblogging about Teaching: Nurturing Participatory Cultures through Collaborative Online Reflection with Pre-Service Teachers," *Teaching and Teacher Education* 40 (2014): 83–93, https://doi.org/10.1016/j.tate.2014.02.002.
26 Arthur L. Costa and Bena Kallick, "Learning and Leading with Habits of Mind: 16 Essential Characteristics for Success," *Association for Supervision and Curriculum Development*, November 30, 2007, https://eric.ed.gov/?id=ED509125.

Bibliography

Brooker, Graeme. "Inner-Propriations: Degrowing the Interior." In *Appropriated Interiors*, edited by, Deborah Schneiderman, Anca I. Lasc, and Karin Tehve, 183–204. New York: Routledge, Taylor & Francis Group, 2022.

Costa, Arthur L., and Bena Kallick. *Learning and Leading with Habits of Mind: 16 Essential Characteristics for Success.* Alexandria: Association for Supervision and Curriculum Development, 2018.

Cross, Ian. "2020 Census: Cleveland, Cuyahoga County Lose Thousands of Residents; Northeast Ohio More Diverse." *News 5 Cleveland WEWS*, August 13, 2021. https://www.news5cleveland.com/news/local-news/2020-census-cleveland-cuyahoga-county-lose-thousands-of-residents-northeast-ohio-more-diverse.

Dewey, John. *Experience and Education.* New York: Free Press, 2015.

Freire, Paulo. *Pedagogy of the Oppressed / Paulo Freire; Translated by Myra Bergman Ramos; with an Introduction by Donaldo Macedo and an Afterword by Ira Shor.* Translated by Myra Bergman Ramos. 50th anniversary ed. New York: Bloomsbury Academic, 2018.

Hadjiyanni, Tasoulla. "Decolonizing Interior Design Education." *Journal of Interior Design* 45, no. 2 (2020): 3–9. https://doi.org/10.1111/joid.12170.

———. "Rethinking Culture in Interior Design Pedagogy: The Potential beyond CIDA Standard 2G." *Journal of Interior Design* 38, no. 3 (2013): 5–12. https://doi.org/10.1111/joid.12013.

Howe, David. Empathy: *What It Is and Why It Matters*. Houndmills, Basingstoke, Hampshire: Palgrave Macmillan, 2013.

Hunt, Roberta. "Service-Learning: An Eye-Opening Experience That Provokes Emotion and Challenges Stereotypes." *Journal of Nursing Education* 46, no. 6 (2007): 277–81. https://doi.org/10.3928/01484834-20070601-07.

Kent State University. "Center for Student Involvement, Resources." 2023. Accessed September 13, 2023. https://www.kent.edu/node/60841.

Krutka, Daniel G., Daniel J. Bergman, Raymond Flores, Katherine Mason, and Ashlie R. Jack. "Microblogging about Teaching: Nurturing Participatory Cultures through Collaborative Online Reflection with Pre-Service Teachers." *Teaching and Teacher Education* 40 (2014): 83–93. https://doi.org/10.1016/j.tate.2014.02.002.

Kwok, P., C. Gill, and P. Chan. " Re-envisioning a Design Curriculum." Paper presented at *DesignEd Asia Conference, Convention and Exhibition Centre*, Hong Kong, 2014.

Larsen, Douglas P., Daniel A. London, and Amanda R. Emke. "Using Reflection to Influence Practice: Student Perceptions of Daily Reflection in Clinical Education." *Perspectives on Medical Education* 5, no. 5 (2016): 285–91. https://doi.org/10.1007/s40037-016-0293-1.

Mattern, Shannon. "Maintenance and Care." *Places Journal*, November 2018. Accessed 27 May 2024. https://doi.org/10.22269/181120.

Matthews, Carl, Ngozi Brown, and Michaela Brooks. "Confronting Lack of Student Diversity in Interior Design Education." *Journal of Interior Design* 46, no. 4 (2021): 3–11. https://doi.org/10.1111/joid.12207.

Media Factual. "The Interior Design Major at Kent State University at Kent." *College Factual*. Accessed September 12, 2023. https://www.collegefactual.com/colleges/kent-state-university-at-kent/academic-life/academic-majors/visual-and-performing-arts/design-and-applied-arts/interior-design/#:~:text=Kent%20State%20Interior%20Design%20Bachelor%27s,men%20and%2097%25%20were%20women.

Otero-Pailos, Jorge. "Monumentaries." In *Tabula Plena: Forms of Urban Preservation*, edited by Bryone Roberts. Zurich: Lars Muller, 2016.

Piotrowski, Christine. *Professional Practice for Interior Designers*. Hoboken, NJ: John Wiley and Sons, Inc., 2020.

Rosaldo, Renato. *Culture & Truth: The Remaking of Social Analysis*. Boston: Beacon Press, 2008.

Tellez-Bohorquez, Fabio. "Empathy Expression and Development in Industrial Design Education." Paper presented in *9th International Conference on Design and Emotion: The Colors of Care*, Universidad de los Andes, Bogota, Columbia, 2014.

Verma, Neeta. "Developing a Pedagogy for Social Design." Paper presented at *The SEGD Academic Summit*, Miami, FL, June 2017.

Yancey, Kathleen Blake. *Reflection in the Writing Classroom*. Boulder, CO: NetLibrary, Inc., 1999.

6 Mismatch

Inclusive Design Strategies Through Pedagogy and Practice

Inge Roecker and Andrea Hoff

Introduction

"At its core, human-[centred] design is about empathizing with people before designing for them."[1]

As we seek new ways for the built environment, particularly that of housing design, to shift and respond to a rapidly changing global environment, the need for equally dramatic change at the core of design culture – in architecture education itself – is a necessary site of introduction. With somewhat surprising resistance, design education has not always been quick to transform. Over three decades ago, Sharon Sutton identified the studio culture of architecture schools as one of the roadblocks to diversifying the profession. Sutton stated that "an exclusionary definition" centered only on aesthetics and disciplinary autonomy that "leaves the choice to become an architect to those few people who wish to practice a 'gentlemanly' art"[2] as a fundamental challenge at the level of pedagogy. Sutton's critique – a direct response to architectural education emerging from modernism which emphasized the importance of theoretical and abstract design principles, often overlooking the practical aspects and lived experiences of buildings and housing in particular – called into the equation not only the built environment but the value systems in place at the heart of design education. Harriss and Widder have since argued that the central emphasis of architecture education needs to move into a model termed as "Live Projects"[3] that addresses the "rising demand for an architecture education that involves distributed authorship, self-advocacy, and other collaboration-based values"[4] and that in this way considers the multiple arenas that architects – especially those engaged in housing design – now encompass. Under this framework, students engage in practical housing design projects that consider not just the visual appeal but also the functional, sustainable and cultural facets of the design.[5]

It is not only the theoretical aspects of design education in need of change but also the structure and hierarchies of how architecture is taught,

DOI: 10.4324/9781032705927-7

the very culture of design education itself. Kathryn Anthony's related research has demonstrated traditional pedagogical methods, such as final reviews and design education studio culture, often undermine rather than contribute to learning outcomes.[6] These design education norms have created a self-perpetuating cycle: design programs often marginalize those students with broader interests, social agendas or unique research interests by continuing to elevate the traditional methods associated with the design studio.

This chapter seeks to document, describe and critique evidence-based teaching and learning strategies for creating new models of design pedagogies and practices. Moreover, the projects presented in this chapter are uniquely suited to the unanticipated rapid change in architecture education that occurred by switching to online learning and hybrid methods as a result of the restrictions associated with the worldwide Covid-19 pandemic. When the primarily in-person education model of the design school had to suddenly transform into an online-based learning environment, design instructors were forced to consider not only new methods of teaching architecture but importantly new ways to connect students to the people and places they were designing for. This provided a unique opportunity to incorporate the social, sustainable and community aspects of design directly within the design brief, as well as to open the conversation up with students on a global scale. The pandemic fundamentally shifted the landscape of design and architecture education, offering new opportunities for equity and access while also raising new challenges related to technology, teaching methods and mental health support. As educational institutions swiftly transitioned to remote learning models, the disparities in access to resources and technology became glaringly evident. This digital divide underscored existing socioeconomic inequities and illuminated the urgent need for more inclusive educational approaches. In terms of instruction, the pandemic catalyzed a shift towards more flexible teaching methods. Faculty were prompted to experiment with asynchronous learning, accommodating students with different schedules, access limitations or time zones. Though not always successful, this turn to asynchronous online learning offered the protential for a more equitable learning environment where students had the opportunity to engage with the material at their own pace. As physical spaces adapted to new health and safety guidelines, students were challenged to rethink architectural design through the larger scope of public health and community well-being. This shift encouraged a more holistic approach to design, emphasizing the creation of inclusive spaces that prioritize the needs of all individuals, including those traditionally marginalized. This chapter presents three projects created by students in the studio, providing a broader reflection on what the practice of centering inclusion can offer to architectural designers at the onset of their careers.

Relevance of Mismatch in Housing

In the frenetic race to offer housing solutions, the valuable qualitative design process that prioritizes and critically involves end-users is minimized or sometimes eliminated altogether. Unfortunately, we recognize a housing crisis better than housing options, which has in turn normalized the current limited accommodation choices. Thus, we often produce housing defined more by financial constraints and marketability instead of the emerging new societal realities and individual needs. When we think of families and individuals at the intersection with other factors such as (dis)ability, poverty and illness, we highlight a demographic of even greater vulnerability. Often marginalized into institutions for decades, these groups have been affected and disenfranchised across many spheres, including access to housing. Along with a lack of design sensitivity, this has resulted in spatial mismatches – creating barriers, often affecting health and social outcomes and increasing isolation and stigmatization. But what are the changes we need in the built environment to promote inclusivity, and how can we understand and design for change? And how can these considerations be supported in the early stages of design education?

This chapter examines how the pedagogy of architecture can foster inclusion as a value system and offer students of architecture the opportunity to develop their skill sets in design that at its very core is centered on inclusion, especially as design education makes a possibly permanent shift initiated by the global pandemic. In addition to the immediate necessity to change how architecture was taught, this dramatic shift opened a view into housing design already off-centered. Housing standards, set out by government and developers, have long neglected people's lived experience, thus creating environments that underserve entire communities.

Given that practice is heavily influenced by the teachings acquired during architecture school, we question: *How does design pedagogy need to change to include lived experience?* A response to this sudden and potentially lasting change was the creation of the housing design class, Mismatch Studio. This chapter examines the reorientation within the Mismatch Studio and also surveys some of the work that the students produced in response. Acting as a case study into how studios such as this one may function and what kinds of work may be produced, this chapter cites exemplars of three projects:

- a multigenerational housing project which included a tofu making factory by Yang Yang (see Figure 6.4);
- a seniors' community residence that could spatially adapt to incorporate family visits, extended stays, as well as age and resulting changing physical abilities by Laura Deacon (see Figure 6.5); and
- a multigenerational co-living facility with an integrated grocery store as residential convenience and collective commercial venture by Robyn Thomson (see Figure 6.6).

Literature Support: Centering Care

> Whilst housing has long been a terrain of struggle in terms of its scale, provision, urban morphology and technological advancement, it often escapes a political critique of its interior logic . . . If most of the newly built stock conforms to models established more than a century ago, an increasing number of "experimental" proposals reimagine domesticity with a chequered success that is surprising if we consider how ill-fitting the petit-bourgeois family flat is to our current conditions.[7]

Care ethics have developed in recent decades as a theory that places the person's relationship to others at the heart of related questions. When we consider the relationships embedded in housing design, as Gutiérrez-Mozo, Parra-Martínez and Gilsanz-Díaz posit in *Extending the Architecture of Collective Housing: Towards Common Worlds of Care*, then we realize that

> [r]ather than a private question, home is a permeable space of great political complexity. It is the product of, among other factors, cultural norms, class rituals, and changing lifestyles. Housing is also the result of multilayered legislations enforcing regulations and building codes, as well as of advertising and commercial practices informing uses and esthetics.[8]

Tracing the development of care ethics in relationship to housing design, we can see that the fundamentals of care as a larger philosophical question arose across disciplines, offering a nuanced reading of the importance of care across the often-siloed academic fields. The drawing together of disciplines (and stakeholders in architecture in particular) is significant when we consider the forces guiding housing design outside of those assumed to be in the immediate realm of architecture, such as planning, politics, economy and other social systems. In the 1980s, Carol Gillian and Nel Noddings developed care ethics as a moral theory separate from other moral imperatives governing human behaviors and decision-making. Though their position has been critiqued in that the ethics of care (as they theorize) is situated in fundamentally women's perspectives and rooted in a binary experience of maternal caring, at the core of their argument is a more expansive sense of care on a human scale, which, in turn, is highly relevant to implications in the built environment. In this more expansive reading of the ethics of care, it can be seen to be part of a larger human network of interdependence and as ingrained in the relationship between people and their well-being. In this way we can see that care ethics as a social theory can function as a reorientation of focus in housing design, from aiming to solve design problems towards caring for people at its core.

When we consider the ethics of care and its focus on the relationships between people,[9] the role of the architectural designer can be understood to bridge the gap between future residents' well-being and the spaces they inhabit. This also implies that when the architect places the needs of the people (the client and future residents) at the heart of the design process, especially those communities who historically have been left out of consideration in this process, the design process and consequently the resulting designs have the possibility to radically shift towards the agency of inhabitants.

As such, the concept of "spatial agency"[10] as defined by Nishat Awan, Tatiana Schneider and Jeremy Till connects the ethics of care and that of agency felt by inhabitants, the feeling of making a difference and the experience of quality of life when considerations of how one lives as connected to what space one inhabits are prioritized in the design process. They identify five realms of influence that have motivated the need to address spatial agency in architecture: politics, the practice, humanitarian crisis, ecology and importantly pedagogy. They speculate (in unison with previously cited Sutton, Harriss and Widder)[11] that the education of architecture has altered little in its core constructs and methodologies since the early days of the École des Beaux Arts of the 19th Century.[12] They surmise that pedagogical practices, such as that of the student and master paradigm, as well as the accepted behavioral norms within architectural education culture – such as persistent sleep deprivation, pitting students against each other, encouraging defensiveness and competition and the raising of certain individuals to pedestals for their designs – has corrupted the potential community-mindedness of the profession at its very developmental stages, that is, in the education of its students.

Though Awan, Schneider and Till acknowledge there have been a number of schools and movements within architecture over the past decade that have attempted to alter these practices, their effect in spatial agency demands an overhaul of the whole system towards one that recognizes the impact that centering the needs of communities can have a great and lasting impact in the field of architecture and on the built environment on a global scale. They call for new pedagogical approaches "in the spirit of mutual knowledge . . . not ones of a prescriptive imposition of knowledge, but of drawing out the vernacular intelligence that the communities already possess".[13] Furthering their agenda and seeing a spark of it in practice, Laurene Vaughan, in conversation with designer Mick Douglas, explores this potential shift in design through care, stating,

> [a] lot of design practice has become more about a practice of being with others. We could say people are becoming the material that we are designing with, whether it is in organizations, communities, or social groupings. Here, the materials are the relationships and the people, and design is a way of manifesting or creating conditions for something to happen.[14]

Shifting the focus towards care has the potential to have dramatic and beneficial impact not only on those who have previously been left out of design discussions but also on the ways in which we can learn through the relationships between people, communities and the world we co-inhabit.

Methodology of the Studio in Context

While architectural and design curricula have clearly transformed in the intervening decades since Sutton's critique of the "gentlemanly arts", the culture of the design schools, teaching methods and role models remain far too similar to the one described by both Sutton and Anthony. Wherein traditional final reviews and critiques, as in earlier models of design education, still tend to foster a culture of hierarchy and judgment that can have negative outcomes. These critiques often prioritize the instructor's or critic's perspective over the student's own vision, potentially stifling creativity and self-expression. This can deter students from exploring innovative, community-oriented housing solutions and in turn can perpetuate an ongoing culture of architectural elitism, wherein the design strategies are still not centering the needs and desires of the future inhabitants. From the very start, this studio aimed to do things differently.

As previously outlined, the studio was entirely online. Students and invited guests joined from locations both local and global, at times synchronously and asynchronously. The studio progressed through iterations of themes and associated exercises, each building upon the knowledge and experience gained by progression. The studio was structured in four cycles of design iterations referred to as "loops", and guests, often from outside the world of architecture, were invited to join the studio via Zoom sessions contributing to weekly workshops, lectures and feedback sessions throughout the term. The learning objectives of the studio were divided into three criteria:

1. To explore emerging inclusive housing typologies and survey existing best practices to create a comparable ground
2. To recognize that engaging in alternative design processes is as important as prototyping the solution
3. To gain an understanding of housing production at the intersection of inclusive housing design

The concept of "loops" of learning was presented in the syllabus and accompanying visualizations, outlining the various steps in the learning cycle and key thematic and methodological elements. The temporal allocations for the course components are represented in the following visual diagram of the studio, as well as guest lectures (represented by speech bubbles in the syntax of comics) and the transformative learning levels moving through storytelling, case study analysis, innovation mapping and designing and prototyping. Each of the iterations are then broken up into two parts, with the final level divided into four parts.

Though a simple addition to the course outline, we found that the accompanying visual outline ensured that course materials were easily navigable (see Figure 6.1). Considering the psychological landscape of the global pandemic,

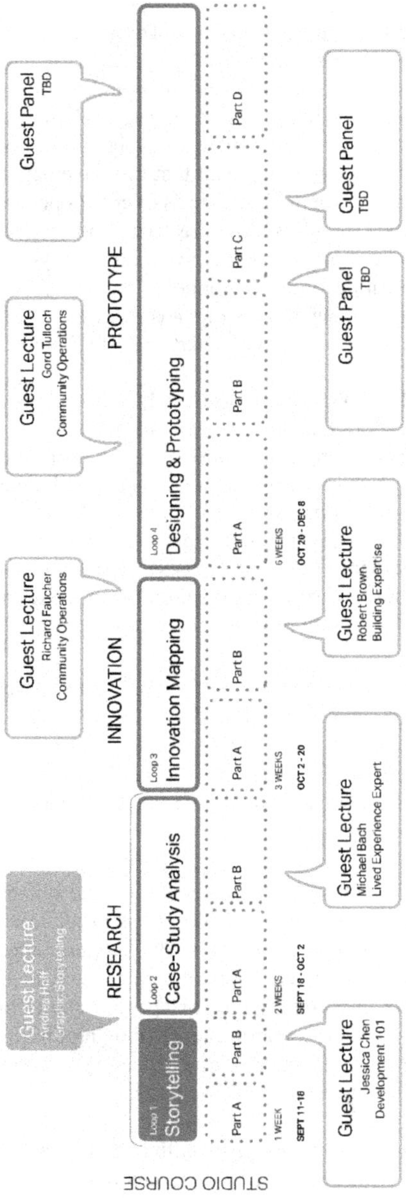

Figure 6.1 Diagram of Mismatch Studio structure, emphasizing the use of loops of learning. Image by authors

as well as the combined synchronous and asynchronous learning environments, we found the visual outline provided students with a roadmap for the entire course, offering clear expectations, deadlines and learning outcomes. We also found it to be a practice that promoted inclusivity by accommodating various learning styles (visual, textual, sequential and narrative) and elevated engagement by making the subject matter more tangible and manageable.

The first step of the design process was a collective immersion in storytelling, and an opportunity from the very start of the studio to bring into awareness the role of the architect in housing design and her/his/their hierarchy of power in the process. As designers, we strive to sharpen our awareness of our own biases before and during the process of design. In the Mismatch Studio, the role of the future residents who will live their lives within the built form was centered in the design process. To understand the complex layers of personal narratives inherent in the people who would hypothetically live in these spaces, it was important from the onset for the students to understand their own positionality and the unique personal narratives they each carry with them as designers.

Through a series of guest lectures and workshops from experts outside of the field of architecture, the use of alternative creative methods in the design process, such as the role of graphic communication, visual storytelling and the concept of design co-creation was offered to students throughout the design process. At the core of this approach was the translation of lived experience through narrative co-creation. In many ways, building this community was possible because of the opportunity to invite guests to present online rather than in person. Civic planners, representatives from disability advocacy organizations, writers, artists and housing activists were all invited to be part of the studio. They joined the class from locations not bound by local geography, in the same way that the students participated from locations around the globe.

One of the initial workshops in the studio involved working with the comics form of storytelling to situate the positionality of the students and bring an awareness to the individual narratives carried equally by designers and by the people for whom they were designing. Following is a set of examples in positionality narratives created by the students, before they began the design process (see Figure 6.2 and Figure 6.3). It was a part of the project that offered students a way to see the complexity of the people and the lives for which they were designing, by interrogating their own personal narratives and positionalities. Each student interviewed another student in the class and created a visual narrative outlining that student's unique personal narrative and the elements in their life that contributed to their positionality. In a larger sense, the positionality exercises aimed to bring to attention designers' self-projection onto the spaces in question and to limit this tendency when it came to design for the intended inhabitants, rather placing inhabitants' needs and desires at the forefront of design decisions.

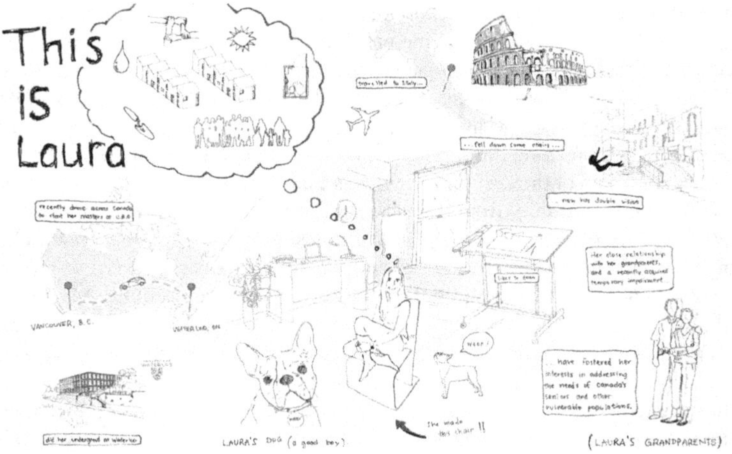

Figure 6.2 Positionality Drawing of Laura Deacon by Andy G.

Figure 6.3 Positionality Drawing of Andy G. by Laura Deacon

The multiple media used in these exercises as well as the varying forms of digital and analog representations is a direct response for more flexible and inclusive educational approaches. Students were encouraged to approach this exercise in ways that were meaningful to them, and in the practice of visual communication to revisit the fundamentals of drawing as a technology, communication and ideas generator. Given the opportunity to choose their media, students worked across divides employing mixed methods and tools such as paper, pen, pencil, paint and digital methods of representation. The resulting images present a unique blend of architectural representation, comics affordances and visual narrative strategies to create highly personal expressions of the multiple stories we each engender within our unique identities.

The studio then immersed the students in a collective research phase in order to question how inclusion can shape home. In teams of two or three, students were asked to discuss the meaning of inclusive housing and asked to contemplate and integrate a series of fundamental questions:

1. How can housing projects adequately deal with human diversity?
2. Where are the opportunities and limits for inclusion in unit design, building design and in the context of the neighborhood?
3. How can we find a balance between the needs and constraints?
4. How can we plan for inclusive housing and communities?
5. How do we instill change in the development process?
6. How can we learn from the experts with lived experiences?
7. What tools and methodologies do we need to learn from the experts with lived experiences?

The teams then presented their findings to the studio and guests as a whole. After these community feedback sessions (different in feel and format from critiques) the teams of students focused on evaluating contemporary models of inclusive housing design with the aim to implement existing methods while innovating strategies on an existing site. This phase offered students the space and time to explore new ideas and concepts before connecting online to a real-world client, the Burnaby Association for Community Inclusion (BACI). BACI then provided the students with two real-world sites and potential program requirements in order to test and expound upon their ideas. In this final phase of the studio, students began working independently to realize their designs and integrated programming. Though the projects from this point on were individual design iterations, the community and comradery of the studio continued to develop, with students seeking input from each other, at times meeting online in smaller groups to discuss and support each other in their designs and community programming integrations.

Project Outcomes of the Studio

The outcomes of the studio were multifaceted, with students exploring multigenerational living configurations aligned with commercial, social and additional community focused ventures. In consideration of the scope and depth of this writing, we focus on three projects from the studio: *Tofu Making + Multi Gen Housing* by Yang (see Figure 6.4); *Adaptable Senior Living* by Laura Deacon (see Figure 6.5); and *Grocery Connecting Community* by Robyn Thomson (see Figure 6.6).

In line with the affirmation that the quality of architecture and quality of life are intertwined, in the writing by Jennifer Molinsky and Ann Forsyth,[15] these projects each sought to focus on the life needs of older adults and on the adaptability of spaces.

> At any age, the pursuit of a good life is easier in a physical environment that promotes health, supports activities important to self-fulfillment, and facilitates connections to the larger community. In old age, the home and neighborhood environments are particularly important: they are the locations where older people spend most their time, and they can [consequently] have a great impact on independence, social connection, feelings of self-worth, and physical and emotional well-being.[16]

Each of the projects highlighted in the following section considered the ways in which real-world multigenerational housing projects are gaining traction as a response to several contemporary societal challenges, including aging populations, housing affordability and environmental sustainability. Each dealt with the design realizations and integration of other services and amenities in unique and creative ways. Importantly, each design proposal originated in the comments, information and presentations presented to the studio by the client group Burnaby Association for Community Inclusion (BACI). BACI, in turn acted as both future tenant (with their new offices housed in the building) and as longtime advocate for the inclusion of underserved groups in society through community living and supportive communities. In essence, the work and values of BACI and the needs of the organization became the design brief for each student's design proposal.

Project One: Tofu Making + Multi Gen Housing

Yang was inspired to integrate a tofu making factory into a multigenerational community to foster a range of benefits, including the promotion of social cohesion and intergenerational interaction (see Figure 6.4). Yang envisioned the community (and commercial) enterprise bringing together people of various age groups, from young children to the elderly. She saw this project as one that could encourage diversity in the exchange of ideas, experiences and knowledge. In the context of a tofu making factory, the potential result also included the transfer of traditional culinary skills from older generations to younger ones. Yang saw the art of tofu production as a unifying activity that could bridge generational gaps and strengthen a sense of community. Moreover, Yang envisioned such a project to promote sustainable living practices. Tofu production typically involves the use of soybeans, a sustainable source of plant-based protein. By producing tofu on-site, the community could reduce its reliance on processed and packaged foods, which often come with a significant carbon footprint. Additionally, the waste generated from tofu production, like okara (soybean pulp), could be repurposed as compost for the community

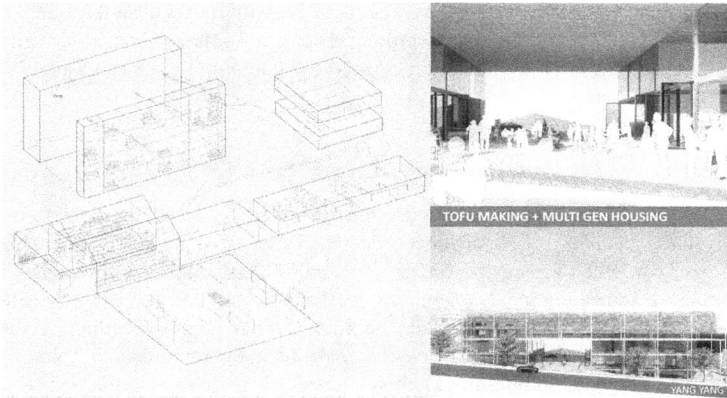

Figure 6.4 Final Project by Yang Yang exploring the center-run sustainable commercial venture of a tofu making facility integrated into the living environment. Drawing by Yang Yang

garden and other communal green spaces, contributing to a circular economy within the community.

Another significant benefit was economic self-sufficiency within the community. The tofu making factory integrated directly into the housing design could serve as a means of income generation for the community, drawing people to the facility and offering employment at all levels of sales, production and distribution. The surplus tofu could be sold locally, thereby supporting the financial well-being of the residents and reducing their reliance on external sources for sustenance. Furthermore, the factory also had the ability to function as an educational center. Residents and employees of the factory could host workshops and classes on tofu production, food sustainability and healthy eating. This learning aspect of the design could not only provide valuable knowledge to the community members but also open doors for external engagement, allowing the community to connect with the broader neighborhood, city and region at large through sharing its sustainable living practices.

In further terms of health and well-being, the presence of a tofu making factory has the potential to promote a nutritious, plant-based diet. Tofu is a versatile, low-fat, high-protein food that fits a variety of dietary preferences, including vegetarian and vegan. By making tofu readily available, the community could encourage its residents to adopt a more sustainable diet. In turn, this could lead to improved overall health outcomes. Another incentive for integrating the tofu making capabilities in the housing design aimed at generating economic revenue for the community. Taking her cue from real-world examples, employment opportunities can be especially beneficial in multigenerational housing projects, as they have the opportunity to cater to different age groups, skills and preferences. The inclusivity in Yang's designs aimed to foster a unique economic empowerment among community members, while building on the strength and interaction of the community members as partners and residents.

Project Two: Adaptable Senior Living

Laura Deacon's project (see Figure 6.5) centered the need for housing to physically adapt as people are encouraged and supported to age in place. This project combined the desire to experience both communal practices, such a preparing and eating meals together as well as the possibility to adapt private living spaces to accommodate adult children, other family members, visiting friends and potentially live-in caregivers. Though communal spaces such as the dining hall, community kitchen and shared gardens encouraged social interaction and collective support for the residents, the individual living units were designed with movable (retracting, sliding and expanding) walls to adapt the configuration of interior spaces to accommodate changes in living support needs while maintaining the privacy of spaces and dignity of the residents. Laura included a visual guide to her designs through integrating a color-coded analysis of highly social, less social and private elements to her schematics.

Project Three: Grocery Connection Community

Robyn Thomson's designs looked at the flow of people and services from the community in the nearby neighborhoods and sought to increase that flow into the multigenerational housing complex (see Figure 6.6). She identified

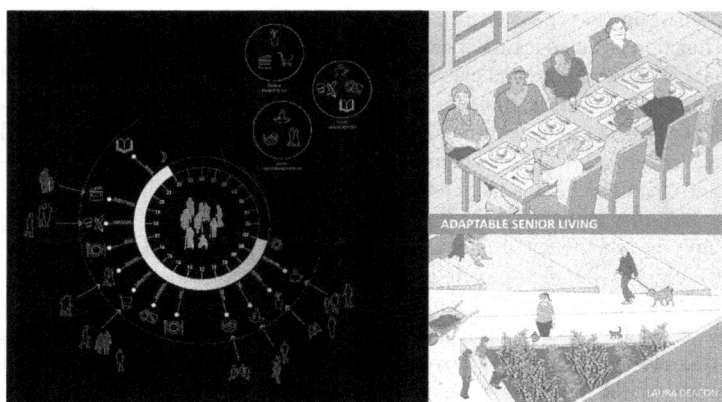

Figure 6.5 Final project by Laura Deacon exploring the different needs of seniors in relationship to adaptable living spaces. Drawing by Laura Deacon

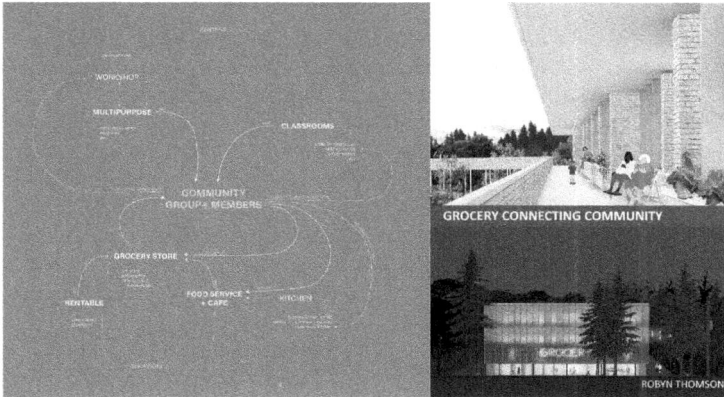

Figure 6.6 Final project by Robyn Thomson exploring the connection between community and commerce with the needs of the community at the center of the design. Drawing by Robyn Thomson

already-in-place amenities and sought to draw both community and commerce to the building through the integration of a grocery store located on the street level of the building. Not only did the introduction of a grocery store provide a needed and unmet amenity to the space, but it also acted as a revenue source for BACI and participating residents. The designs for the housing elements further integrated the flow of people, balanced the need for both private and public spaces and provided opportunities for neighbors to meet with each other and experience small spaces of regular interaction on all floors of the building (as can be seen in the far right of Figure 6.6, depicting the small spaces of interaction). The grocery store also worked to provide the nieghborhood with an unmet amenity, leading to the development of other social enterprise endeavors such as an adjoining café, community rental spaces for events and workshops, a multipurpose space and the opportunity to convert open areas into classroom environments, providing space for multigenerational learning interactions and shared creative practices.

As case studies, uniquely situated in the sudden design reorientation (due in part to restrictions caused by the global pandemic), these projects each center on community inclusion, sustainability and multigenerational housing as both a design practice and a theoretical framework. Though significantly different in terms of design articulation, each project imagines the interconnection of support, services and community at the core of the built environment. What becomes clear when returning to the objectives of the studio – particularly the initial studio discussions on how housing projects can adequately deal with human diversity and how we, as designers, can instill change in the development process – each project clearly reorientates inclusion in the unit design, building design and in the context of the neighborhood. What appears at first to be a whimsical design decision, such as integrating a tofu production facility (see Figure 6.4) into a multigenerational housing development can be seen through the lens of inclusion to be a thoughtful and highly creative strategy to support intergenerational learning, connection and self-sustainability. The simple design moves of integrating a grocery store into multiunit housing (see Figure 6.6) and designing for adjustable interior wall configurations (see Figure 6.5) both prioritize the collective needs expressed by the future inhabitants. The diversity of these projects speak to the multiple ways in which emerging designers in the Mismatch Studio were emboldened to listen and learn from the experts with lived experiences, and to consider what life could be like and what lives could be lived within these designs.

Conclusion and Future Directions

We live in an era of accelerated change. World demographics and social constructs have altered drastically during the last century, and even more rapidly over the past three years. With this shift, whether voluntary or involuntary, lifestyles are becoming increasingly virtual, mobile and unstable. Even though today's world is more diverse, housing and the way it is procured appears to be stuck in a different and incompatible era. At the dawn of modernity, the goal to innovate for a universal humanity was propelled by a scientific process that could streamline every process, design included. This universality was essentially characterized in the 20th century as a world tailored for the middle-class, white, heterosexual man. We do not inhabit this atavistic version of the world.

We find ourselves in a time of unprecedented societal transformation. The traditional notions of family, relationships and community have evolved significantly. People are now choosing to live alone for more extended periods, delaying marriage or not marrying at all, and opting for smaller families. This shift, whether driven by choice or circumstance, is reshaping our lifestyles to be more virtual, mobile and transient. However, our approach to housing and its procurement seems to lag behind, firmly rooted in a bygone era. In fact, as Subrahmanian, Reich and Krishnan explain, "we have sculpted the world we inhabit extensively, and what ails us is a dissonance of our own making. The dialogue between us – the one between the material world of our creation and the natural world – lies broken because the dialogue in designing this world of our creation is broken".[17]

As design instructors, we carry an ethical responsibility to confront these incompatibilities while addressing the fundamental need for shelter. The ideal vision is a reimagining of housing, where it is versatile, accessible, and responsive to the diverse experiences and needs of its inhabitants. The focus of design should be to provide a fundamental right to housing that acknowledges the unique needs of each individual. With these principles in mind, the efforts within this studio and the broader transformation of architectural design pedagogy aim to reclaim design as a field where humanity takes center stage. It is a space where various perspectives converge to shape the world we inhabit. The adjustments made in response to the challenges posed by the pandemic initiated this transformation. The future now lies in the balance, with the choice to either revert to the status quo or embrace a forward-looking approach that considers the well-being of both the future and the individuals involved. The transformation needs to involve reimagining design as a collaborative process. And it needs to empower people to become active participants in the creation of the built environment. We believe this transformation must start at the very foundation of architectural education, where we can nurture a generation of architects who are not only mindful of the pressing needs of humanity but actively engaged in shaping a better, more inclusive world through their designs.

With this in mind, our efforts through this studio – and the recalibration of practices within architectural design pedagogy – are to reclaim design as "a field of practice where people are the focus, where different perspectives can come together and shape the world".[18] The imposed modifications to how we taught during the pandemic initiated this transformation; what we do with it from here will be determined either by the decision to return to how things were or to go forward with care for the future, for each other and for how we position ourselves as architects designing for a better world. And like Subrahmanian, Reich and Krishnan, "we reimagine designing in a way that people are not reduced to being mere users but become a part of the process – active participants in the designing and creation of an artifact".[19] And we believe that this transformation has the potential to take root where the pedagogy of architecture first manifests in the design classroom.

Acknowledgments

We would like to thank the Master of Architecture students at the University of British Columbia who took part in the Mismatch Studio. We are especially grateful to Laura Deacon, Andy G., Robyn Thomson, and Yang Yang for including their engaging and thoughtful work in this chapter.

Research for this chapter is supported in part by funding from the Social Sciences and Humanities Research Council of Canada.

Conseil de recherches en sciences humaines du Canada   Social Sciences and Humanities Research Council of Canada   Canada

Notes

1 Sina Mossayeb, "Foreword: Closing the Gap between the Designer and the Recipients of Design," in *Diversity and Design: Understanding Hidden Consequences*, ed. Tauke, Beth, Korydon Smith, and Charles Davis, xvii. Book, Whole (London: Routledge, 2016), https://doi.org/10.4324/9781315775791
2 Sutton, Sharon E., Susan P. Kemp, and Palgrave Social Sciences Collection, *The Paradox of Urban Space: Inequality and Transformation in Marginalized Communities,* 1st ed. (New York: Palgrave Macmillan, 2011), https://doi.org/10.1057/9780230117204.
3 In essence, the concept of "Live Projects" seeks to address a comprehensive understanding of the human element in housing by bringing students into direct contact with clients, communities and the socio-cultural context in which housing exists. It achieves this by involving students directly with clients, communities and the socio-cultural environment in which housing is situated.
4 Harriet Harriss and Lynnette Widder, *Architecture Live Projects: Pedagogy into Practice* (New York, NY: Taylor and Francis, 2014), 1.
5 This approach places a higher emphasis on a holistic understanding of housing, which encompasses the diverse requirements and aspirations of the individuals who will ultimately live in these spaces.
6 Kathryn H. Anthony, "Designing for Diversity: Implications for Architectural Education in the Twenty-First Century," *Journal of Architectural Education (1984)* 55, no. 4 (2002): 257–67.
7 Maria S. Giudici, "Counter-Planning from the Kitchen: For a Feminist Critique of Type," *Journal of Architecture (London, England)* 23, no. 7–8 (2018): 1203.
8 María-Elia Gutiérrez-Mozo, José Parra-Martínez, and Ana Gilsanz-Díaz, "Extending the Architecture of Collective Housing: Towards Common Worlds of Care," *Buildings (Basel)* 11, no. 4 (2021): 166.
9 Joan C. Tronto, "Beyond Gender Difference to a Theory of Care," *Signs* 12, no. 4 (1987): 644–63, http://www.jstor.org/stable/3174207.
10 Nishat Awan, Tatjana Schneider, and Jeremy Till, *Spatial Agency: Other Ways of Doing Architecture* (Abingdon, Oxon [England]; New York, NY: Routledge, 2011; 2013).
11 Harriss and Widder, *Architecture Live Projects*.
12 Awan et al., *Spatial Agency*, 46.
13 Ibid., 48.
14 Mick Douglas and Laurene Vaughan, "Performing a Practice of Care: A Dialogue," in *Designing Cultures of Care,* ed. Laurene Vaughan (London: Bloomsbury Academic, 2019), 222.
15 Jennifer Molinsky and Ann Forsyth, "Housing, the Built Environment, and the Good Life," *The Hastings Center Report* 48, no. S3 (2018).
16 Ibid., S51.
17 Eswaran Subrahmanian, Yoram Reich, and Sruthi Krishnan, *We Are Not Users* (Cambridge: The MIT Press, 2020), 7.
18 Ibid.
19 Ibid., 6.

Bibliography

Anthony, Kathryn H. "Built-in Bias." *The Architectural Review* 243, no. 1449 (2018): 29.

———. *Designing for Diversity: Gender, Race, and Ethnicity in the Architectural Profession.* Urbana: University of Illinois Press, 2001.

———. "Designing for Diversity: Implications for Architectural Education in the Twenty-First Century." *Journal of Architectural Education (1984)* 55, no. 4 (2002): 257–67. https://doi.org/10.1162/104648802753657969.

Awan, Nishat. *Diasporic Agencies: Mapping the City Otherwise.* 1st ed. Book, Whole. Farnham Surrey, England; Burlington, VT: Ashgate Publishing Company, 2016. https://doi.org/10.4324/9781315577029.

Awan, Nishat, Tatjana Schneider, and Jeremy Till. *Spatial Agency: Other Ways of Doing Architecture.* Book, Whole. Abingdon, Oxon [England]; New York, NY: Routledge, 2011. https://doi.org/10.4324/9781315881249.

Charbonneau, Johanne. "WALKER, Margaret Urban. 1998. Moral Understandings. A Feminist Study in Ethics. New York, Routledge. CLEMENT, Grace. 1996. Care, Autonomy and Justice. Feminism and the Ethic of Care. Boulder, Co., Westview Press. LAMB, Sharon. 1996. The Trouble with Blame. Victims, Perpetrators and Responsibility. Cambridge, MA, et Londres, G.-B., Harvard University Press." *Lien social et politiques*, no. 46 (2001): 175. https://doi.org/10.7202/000332ar.

Clement, Grace. *Care, Autonomy, and Justice: Feminism and the Ethic of Care.* Book, Whole. New York: Routledge, 2018. https://doi.org/10.4324/9780429501838.

Costanza-Chock, Sasha, Megan Tusing, and O'Reilly for Higher Education. *Design Justice.* Book, Whole. Old Saybrook, CT: Tantor Media, Inc., 2021.

Douglas, Mick, and Laurene Vaughan. "Performing a Practice of Care: A Dialogue." In *Designing Cultures of Care*, edited by Laurene Vaughan, 1st ed., 221–28. London: Bloomsbury Academic, 2019.

Engineer, Altaf, and Kathryn H. Anthony. *Shedding New Light on Art Museum Additions: Front Stage and Back Stage Experiences.* 1st ed. Book, Whole. London: Routledge, 2018. https://doi.org/10.4324/9781315443164.

Giudici, Maria S. "Counter-Planning from the Kitchen: For a Feminist Critique of Type." *Journal of Architecture (London, England)* 23, no. 7–8 (2018): 1203–29. https://doi.org/10.1080/13602365.2018.1513417.

Gürel, Meltem Ö., and Kathryn H. Anthony. "The Canon and the Void: Gender, Race, and Architectural History Texts." *Journal of Architectural Education (1984)* 59, no. 3 (2006): 66–76.

Gutiérrez-Mozo, María-Elia, José Parra-Martínez, and Ana Gilsanz-Díaz. "Extending the Architecture of Collective Housing: Towards Common Worlds of Care." *Buildings (Basel)* 11, no. 4 (2021): 166. https://doi.org/10.3390/buildings11040166.

Harriss, Harriet, and Lynnette Widder. *Architecture Live Projects: Pedagogy into Practice.* Book, Whole. New York, NY: Taylor and Francis, 2014. https://doi.org/10.4324/9781315780764.

Jackson Bell, Carla. *Space Unveiled: Invisible Cultures in the Design Studio.* Book, Whole. London: Routledge, 2015. https://doi.org/10.4324/9781315765990.

Molinsky, Jennifer, and Ann Forsyth. "Housing, the Built Environment, and the Good Life." *The Hastings Center Report* 48, no. S3 (2018): S50–56. https://doi.org/10.1002/hast.914.

Mossayeb, Sina. "Foreword: Closing the Gap between the Designer and the Recipients of Design." In *Diversity and Design: Understanding Hidden Consequences*, edited by Beth Tauke, Korydon Smith, and Charles Davis, xvii–xix. Book, Whole. London: Routledge, 2016. https://doi.org/10.4324/9781315775791.

Noddings, Nel. "Care, Autonomy, and Justice: Feminism and the Ethic of Care." *Ethics* 108, no. 3 (1998): 655–656.

Subrahmanian, Eswaran, Yoram Reich, and Sruthi Krishnan. *We Are Not Users*. Book, Whole. Cambridge: The MIT Press, 2020. https://doi.org/10.7551/mitpress/11931.001.0001.

Sutton, Damian, Susan Brind, and Ray McKenzie. *The State of the Real: Aesthetics in the Digital Age*. Book, Whole. London; New York: I.B. Tauris, 2007. https://go.exlibris.link/hwt6xqS1.

Sutton, Sharon E., and Susan P. Kemp, and Palgrave Social Sciences Collection. *The Paradox of Urban Space: Inequality and Transformation in Marginalized Communities*. 1st ed. Book, Whole. New York: Palgrave Macmillan, 2011. https://doi.org/10.1057/9780230117204.

Tauke, Beth, Korydon Smith, and Charles Davis. *Diversity and Design: Understanding Hidden Consequences*. Book, Whole. London: Routledge, 2016. https://doi.org/10.4324/9781315775791.

Tironi, Martín. "Ethics of Care of Urban Resources: Maintenance and Repair on a Public Bicycle System." *ARQ (Santiago, Chile)*, no. 89 (2015): 76–89. https://doi.org/10.4067/S0717-69962015000100011.

Tronto, Joan C. "Beyond Gender Difference to a Theory of Care." *Signs* 12, no. 4 (1987): 644–63.

Vaughan, Laurene and Bloomsbury Collections: All Titles. *Designing Cultures of Care*. 1st ed. Book, Whole. London, England: Bloomsbury Publishing, 2018 https://doi.org/10.5040/9781350055391.

Index

Note: Page numbers in *italics* indicate a figure on the corresponding page.

For Product Safety Concerns and Information please contact our EU
representative GPSR@taylorandfrancis.com
Taylor & Francis Verlag GmbH, Kaufingerstraße 24, 80331 München, Germany

www.ingramcontent.com/pod-product-compliance
Lightning Source LLC
Chambersburg PA
CBHW061744270326
41928CB00011B/2362